CAMBRIDGE FIRST CERTIFIC
Series editor: Sue O'Connell

KT-388-866

CAMBRIDGE FIRST CERTIFICATE
Writing

Richard MacAndrew
Cathy Lawday

CAMBRIDGE
UNIVERSITY PRESS

Published by the Press Syndicate of the University of Cambridge
The Pitt Building, Trumpington Street, Cambridge CB2 1RP
40 West 20th Street, New York, NY 10011–4211, USA
10 Stamford Road, Oakleigh, Melbourne 3166, Australia

Reprinted 1994

Richard MacAndrew and Cathy Lawday have asserted their
right to be identified as the Authors of the Work in accordance
with the Copyright, Design and Patents Act 1988.

First published 1993

Printed in Great Britain by Scotprint Ltd

ISBN 0 521 40900 4 Student's Book
ISBN 0 521 40901 2 Teacher's Book

WD

Contents

Map of the book

	Topic	Planning	Improving
	Foundation unit	What are your expectations? What sorts of writing does the First Certificate exam require?	
1	**A funny thing happened** anecdotes	ordering events 'flow diagram'	checking and polishing
2	**Wage slaves** work	deciding priorities	organising your work
3	**On the road** travel	listing questions (letter layout)	self-assessment 1
4	**A tall, dark, handsome stranger** people	using a 'spidergraph'	adding interest and personalisation
5	**Through the grapevine** media	listing advantages and disadvantages	what we write
6	**Being green** environment	using a questionnaire	why we write
7	**Learn a language** language learning	'brainstorming'	clear handwriting
8	**Bestsellers** books	selecting relevant information	using resources
9	**Family life** family	using 'headlights'	learning useful expressions
10	**A roof over your head** houses	using a questionnaire	self-assessment 2
11	**Jobhunting** jobs	listing questions	planning in the exam
12	**Getaway** holidays	using a 'spidergraph'	checking and polishing in the exam
13	**Crime doesn't pay** crime	opening sentences	writing the correct number of words in the exam
14	**Good sports** sport and leisure	deciding priorities	reading and answering the question
15	**Customer relations** services	selecting relevant information	brief and accurate writing
16	**Eat it!** food	'brainstorming'	managing time in the exam
17	**Stay healthy!** health	using boxes for categories	checking in the exam
18	**A birthday book** gifts and books	review of planning techniques	the future
	Review unit	How much do you know about the exam? How much do you remember about planning?	

Exam question	Skills 1	Skills 2
What does the First Certificate exam expect? How do 'good' writers write? How can I evaluate and improve my work?		
paper 2: narrative	past tenses	time linking words
paper 3: directed writing	selecting relevant information	giving and justifying opinions
paper 2: informal letter	giving advice	punctuating correctly
paper 2: description	adjectives for describing people	ordering adjectives
paper 2: discussion essay	paragraphing	talking about advantages and disadvantages
paper 3: directed writing	evaluating information	linking words for reasons and results
paper 2: formal letter	letter-writing rules	making requests
paper 2: speech	characteristics of spoken language	expressing attitude
paper 2: discussion essay	opening and closing paragraphs	recognising how a text links together
paper 3: directed writing	interpreting abbreviations	expanding and rephrasing information
paper 2: formal letter	recognising topic and illustrative sentences	making applications
paper 2: description	organising descriptions	prepositions following adjectives
paper 2: narrative	using direct speech in narratives	making your writing more interesting
paper 3: directed writing	combining information	verbs which take the gerund and/or infinitive
paper 2: formal letter	linking words for attitude	the past in sequence
paper 2: speech	giving instructions	linking words for instructions
paper 2: discussion essay	writing a paragraph	inversion
paper 3: directed writing	making difficult choices	relative clauses

How much do you remember about the Exam Tips? How prepared are you?
How good are you at polishing your work?

Acknowledgements

We would like to thank the Series Editor, Sue O'Connell, for her invaluable help and guidance, our editor Jeanne McCarten for nursing authors and manuscript through all the various stages, Geraldine Mark, Joanne Currie and the staff at Cambridge University Press for their efforts in the production of the book, and of course the teachers and students who piloted it, for their helpful comments.

The authors and publishers are grateful to the following individuals and institutions for permission to use copyright material in *Cambridge First Certificate Writing*. While every effort has been made, it has not been possible to identify the sources of all the material used and in such cases the publishers would welcome information from copyright holders.

Cartoons

Geoff Thompson: pp. 11 and 36; *Private Eye*: pp. 18, 41, 53, 58, 68, 82, 87 and 99; *The Spectator*: pp. 21, 29, 34, 49, 63, 76 and 92.

Photographs

Sally and Richard Greenhill Photolibrary: p. 26; Sony: p. 33; Panos Pictures: pp. 37, 39 and 75; Pocock and Shaw, Cambridge: pp. 63 and 65 (1, 2, 4 and 5); Bernard Payne: p. 65 (houseboat); Thames Television for the picture from the television series *Something in Disguise*: p. 109.

Text extracts

Paladin, an imprint of HarperCollins Publishers Limited for the extract from *Danziger's Travels* by Nick Danziger: p. 75; The Peters, Fraser & Dunlop Group for the extract from *The Veiled One* by Ruth Rendell: p. 79 (A); Virgin Publishing for the extract from *Meet Me At the Morgue* by Ross MacDonald: p.79 (B); William Heinemann for the extract from *The Mysterious Mr Ripley* by Patricia Highsmith: p. 79 (C); David Bolt Associates for the extract from *The Janus Murder Case* by Colin Wilson: p. 80; Macmillan London Limited for the extract from *Last Seen Wearing* by Colin Dexter: p. 81; Penguin Books Limited for the back cover of *Something in Disguise* by Elizabeth Jane Howard: p. 109.

Illustrations

Nigel Paige: pp. 6, 12, 55, 57, 91 and 104; Amanda MacPhail: pp. 10, 13 (bottom), 14, 15, 17, 20, 23, 24 (top), 25, 27, 31, 32, 33, 38, 40, 44, 45, 47, 51, 53, 54, 56, 60, 61, 71, 73, 76, 82, 83, 90, 93, 96, 99, 101, 103, 105, 106, 108, 111 and 114; Peter Byatt: pp. 13 (top), 22 and 97; Joanne Currie: pp. 15, 16 and 38; Helen Humphries: pp. 24 (bottom), 27 (top), 42, 58, 74 and 94; Helena Greene: pp. 98 and 100.

Cover illustration by Annabel Wright

Introduction

Who is this book for?

This book provides writing practice for students preparing for the writing components of the Cambridge FCE exam: Paper 2 (Composition) and the directed writing section of Paper 3. It may also be used as a general writing skills course at this level. It aims to provide both skills development and exam training; to cover a wide range of topics and functions; to draw students' attention to the 'process' of writing – through the stages of planning, writing and improving; to give interesting, motivating tasks.

How is the book organised?

The book is organised into eighteen units. Each unit focuses on a particular type of First Certificate question and concentrates on the language and writing skills students will need to answer that question.

How is each unit organised?

Each unit starts with a **preview** section introducing the topic dealt with in the unit.

This is followed by a **planning** section which introduces students to one of a variety of planning techniques which they are encouraged to experiment with throughout the course.

Two **skills development** sections follow, providing practice in language and writing skills that students will find useful in performing the writing task.

A further **planning** section gives students the opportunity to put into practice the technique learnt earlier in the unit. This second section can be done in class or, if time is short, for homework along with the exam question.

An **exam-type question**, for use either in class or as homework, provides realistic First Certificate practice.

The unit is completed with an **improving your work** section to be tackled after the writing task is finished. This section encourages students to revise and polish their work. It also gives practical learner training ideas and activities both to help students prepare specifically for the exam and to enable them to develop their writing and general language learning skills.

How should the material be used?

The course may be used in strict unit sequence. Alternatively teachers may wish to develop each exam question type in sequence.

Each unit provides about an hour's pre-task work. There is scope for flexibility, however, and the Teacher's Book suggests ways of extending or reducing the time needed. The exam-type question can be done either in class or for homework. Timed practices of 45 minutes will be necessary towards the exam. The improving section should be done in a follow-up lesson and will take 15–20 minutes depending on the task and how it develops.

What special features are there?

* The book begins with a **Foundation unit** which is designed to increase students' awareness of key aspects of writing.

* Each unit begins with a **mini-syllabus** to show students exactly which type of exam question and which skills are covered in the unit.

* Each unit contains **Exam Tips** which summarise key points to remember for the exam. Some units also contain **Study Tips** which give useful advice on how to improve your writing generally.

* The detailed **Teacher's Book** provides practical suggestions, ideas for further activities, and guidelines on timing.

* The book finishes with a **Review unit** which brings together as much essential information as possible for a final revision session.

Foundation unit

What are your expectations?

What do you expect to learn from a writing skills course? Read and discuss these comments from students.

1 I would like to learn more grammar and vocabulary to improve my writing.

2 I would like to learn how to plan and write a composition.

3 I would like to communicate more clearly and expressively through my writing.

4 I would like to learn the differences in style between written English and spoken English.

5 When I go to a writing course I expect to learn to write good English – not Norwegian English.

6 I would like to learn how to spell and punctuate correctly.

7 I'd like to learn how and what to write on different occasions, the right tone, how to start, how to finish, etc.

8 I would like to learn the kind of vocabulary necessary in each case (for example, in a complaining letter, in a report, in a story, etc.

9 I want to pass the First Certificate, so I need to practise the kinds of writing for that.

10 I'd like to learn some techniques which will help me improve my writing.

Which points are important to you?

What sorts of writing does the First Certificate exam require?

For Paper 2 of the First Certificate exam you have to write:

two compositions

of 120–180 words

in 1½ hours.

You should be able to produce different forms of writing:

letters (both formal and informal)

speeches   →   writing a text of (often informal) spoken English

formal compositions: narrative   →   telling a story

                   descriptive   →   describing a person or place

                   discussion essay   →   putting forward an idea or argument

You may also write about one of the set books.

In Paper 3 of the exam there is a directed writing exercise for which you should allow approximately 30 minutes. For this task you need to be able to use different skills (e.g. selecting, evaluating or combining information) in order to produce three or four paragraphs totalling 150–200 words.

Look at the extracts below and decide which form of writing they are. Some extracts may have more than one possible answer.

informal letter   formal letter   narrative

discussion essay   description   speech

1   When we had gone about three or four miles, the engine suddenly started to make strange noises. Eventually it stopped completely. I looked at the petrol gauge. I thought to myself, 'Oh no! No petrol!'

2   It was a pity you couldn't get to Harry's party as I'm sure you'd have enjoyed it. It was great fun and we all had a wonderful time.

3   We have two bedrooms and a bathroom upstairs, and a kitchen, a dining-room and a living room. My favourite room is the kitchen: it is a large, airy room with a beautiful view over our garden.

4 Jill has not only been an excellent member of our management team; she has been a good friend & colleague for the last 25 years.

5 I think he's quite attractive. He's tall with dark hair and a moustache, and he's got a great sense of humour. You'll really enjoy meeting him when you come over.

6 One advantage of living alone is that you never have arguments over who does the washing up. Another is that you can always watch what you want on TV.

7 My friend and I are very interested in your Three Peaks Tour and would be grateful if you would send us further information.

What does the First Certificate exam expect?

Which do you think are the most important factors when writing? Pick the four most important from the list below and compare your answer with a partner.

spelling correctly
using correct grammar
answering the question fully
using correct punctuation
writing the correct number of words
writing legibly
using a wide range of vocabulary
writing relevant answers

How do 'good' writers write?

1 You have offered to write an article for an English language magazine in your country. Look at the seven stages below which show the process of planning and writing. Work in pairs and number the stages to show how you think the writing process works.

making a rough outline or plan
revising and redrafting the article
having an idea you want to write about
making out a neat copy ready for publishing
making notes on the topic
getting your ideas together
writing a first draft

2 Which of these pieces of writing would you plan very carefully and which would you plan less carefully? Mark them *C* for carefully planned, *P* for planned or *U* for unplanned.

> birthday card to a friend
> letter to your American penfriend
> postcard to your family
> short story
> note to a close friend
> letter applying for a job in Australia
> notes for a speech at a wedding
> English exam composition: 'Things I like to do'
> letter of complaint to a mail order company
> note to pin to your door while you go out
> love letter

3 How would you change the order of the stages in exercise 1 above to show how the writing process works for an exam composition?

Remember – very little writing is totally unplanned. Even on a simple birthday card to a friend we may spend some time thinking of something amusing, revising our ideas a few times before finally putting pen to paper.

How can I evaluate and improve my work?

Do you agree or disagree with the statements below? Work on your own first, then compare your answers with other people in the class.

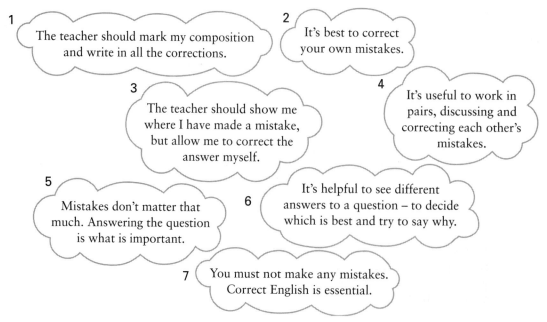

1 The teacher should mark my composition and write in all the corrections.

2 It's best to correct your own mistakes.

3 The teacher should show me where I have made a mistake, but allow me to correct the answer myself.

4 It's useful to work in pairs, discussing and correcting each other's mistakes.

5 Mistakes don't matter that much. Answering the question is what is important.

6 It's helpful to see different answers to a question – to decide which is best and try to say why.

7 You must not make any mistakes. Correct English is essential.

One way of helping you learn to correct your own work is to use a correction code. Look at the code below and fill in the gaps.

Correction code

Symbol	Meaning	Wrong	Right
Sp	spelling	tabel	....
P	punctuation/capitals	i speak english	....
T	verb/tense	He come yesterday.	....
N	number	She watch TV.	....
F	form	This book is bored.	....
WO	word order	I like very much eggs.	....
WW	....	Today it's shiny.	Today's it's sunny.
G	grammar	He doesn't listened.	....
A	....	He's at the work.	He's at work.
λ	omission	He tall.	....
/	word too many	It's the his book.	....
//	paragraphing		
N/A	not appropriate wrong register	Dear Sir/Madam, Send me information	....
?	don't understand		
~~	not quite right		
✓	good		

Unit 1 A funny thing happened

Planning technique:	ordering events; 'flow diagram'
Language skills:	past tenses; time linking words
Exam question:	paper 2: narrative
Improving:	checking and polishing

Preview

Work in pairs. Choose one of the subjects below and tell your partner about it.

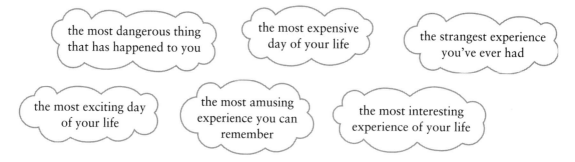

the most dangerous thing that has happened to you

the most expensive day of your life

the strangest experience you've ever had

the most exciting day of your life

the most amusing experience you can remember

the most interesting experience of your life

Planning 1

Read this letter and do the activities below it.

Dear Jo,

Greetings from the round-the-world travellers. Thanks for your letter & Christmas card which we got just before we left the Philippines. It was great to hear from you.

We're having a wonderful time, but we've had some nervous moments. We had a memorable flight just before Christmas. This is what happened. We had just spent three weeks on the beautiful island of Boracay where we had been renting a bamboo hut on the beach for £1 a night. Paradise! However, we had to be back in Manila by Christmas so we booked a flight in a private plane.

It was a typical tropical morning, hot & humid. We walked along the beach to meet Roger, who had organised the flight, & the other passengers. Roger introduced us to everybody & then we took the small boat across to Caticlan on the island of Panay. When we arrived there we were taken to the airstrip where the plane was already waiting.

After a short time the pilot arrived. We were introduced to him as well (the service was much more friendly than British Airways!) & quite soon afterwards we took off. At first I was a bit worried about flying in such a small aircraft. However, after we had taken off I forgot my worries. I just enjoyed the views as we flew over some of the most spectacular scenery in South-East Asia.

Finally, at about 12 o'clock we began to descend towards Manila Airport. The pilot was talking on the radio to the control tower while he brought the plane down gently towards the runway. Suddenly, he announced that the transmission had failed. I looked round for a parachute but there wasn't one. However, nothing terrible seemed to happen & the pilot didn't seem worried. Eventually I realised that he meant the radio transmission & not something to do with the engine. We landed safely a few minutes later. I must admit I'm not very happy about flying in big planes, as for little ones — never again!

Hope you're well. See you in a few months — perhaps with some more 'exciting' tales!

Love, Robin

1 Work in pairs. Which four paragraphs in the letter tell the story?

2 Put the sentences below in the correct order to match the story, then write them in the boxes to give yourself a complete diagram. This is called a 'flow diagram'.

The pilot arrived.	1	We had been staying on Boracay
		↓
We met the other passengers.	2	
		↓
The transmission failed.	3	
		↓
The plane took off.	4	
		↓
We had been staying on Boracay.	5	
		↓
We went to the airstrip.	6	
		↓
We booked a flight.	7	
		↓
We landed at Manila.	8	
		↓
The pilot spoke on the radio.	9	

EXAM TIP 1

A 'flow diagram' is a useful way of planning a **narrative** composition or any other piece of writing which describes a sequence of events. Note down random ideas and arrange them in order before beginning to write.

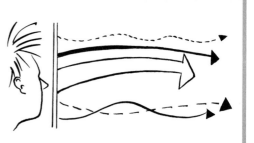

3 Now match the headings on the right to the paragraphs in the story on pages 8 and 9.

Para 1 .... first events
Para 2 .... final events and outcome
Para 3 .... background
Para 4 .... later events

EXAM TIP 2

Remember this paragraph order when you want to plan a narrative composition or any story.

You can even do this with very short stories, e.g. I was walking along the street on my way to work (*background*) when a dog ran in front of me (*first events*). I was watching the dog (*later events*) and stepped into a huge puddle (*final events and outcome*).

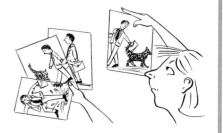

Past tenses

1 Look at this table. Fill in the *Use* column from the explanations below the table. Fill in the *Examples* column with examples from the text in Planning 1.

Tense	Use	Examples
Past simple	....	....
Past continuous	....	....
Past perfect	....	....
Past perfect continuous	....	....

a) We use this form to emphasise the duration of an action/state in the past.
b) If we are already talking about the past, we use this form to refer to an earlier past time.
c) We use this form to emphasise the duration of actions/states which occurred continuously up to the past moment we are thinking about.
d) We use this form to talk about an action/state at a particular time in the past.

2 Put the verbs in brackets in the correct past tense in the text below.

My most frightening experience .... (be) once when we ....
.... (walk) in Scotland. We .... (start) out at six o'clock
in the morning and .... (go) for three hours when suddenly the fog
.... (come) down. A few moments earlier we ....
(be able) to see the top of the mountain and the village where we ....
(spend) the night. Now we .... (can) only just see a tree twenty metres away.
We .... (stop) to get out the map and compass and .... (make) an
awful discovery. I .... (leave) the compass on the table in our hotel room.

Time linking words

1 Find all the time linking words and phrases in the text in Planning 1 and list them below.

then
when

'Cross? I'm absolutely furious.'

2 **Cross out the words or phrases which could not be used in the following sentences. There may be more than one correct possibility.**

About three years ago I had a job as a sales representative. I travelled all over the country

visiting different shops. One day
when
as
then
(1) I was driving along some deserted country

roads, my car
suddenly
eventually
afterwards
(2) started making a strange noise.
When
At first
After
(3) I thought it was

the engine; but
then
quite soon afterwards
when
(4) it started to bump along the road and I realised I

had a flat tyre. I stopped to change the wheel. The jack was old and didn't work very well, but

eventually
finally
then
(5) I managed to get the wheel off.
A few minutes later
Quite soon afterwards
After
(6),
as
while
when
(7)

I was putting the spare tyre on, another car stopped behind me. The driver got out, with his

own jack, came over and started lifting up the other side of my car.
After
When
Afterwards
(8) he had

got it about 30 cm off the ground, I went round and asked him what he was doing. 'You take

those two wheels and I'll take these two,' he said. He left very quickly
when
then
finally
(9) he

discovered it was my car!

Compare your answers with a partner.

Planning 2

Look at these pictures. Work in pairs to make up a story which involves all the items drawn below. Organise the main events in a 'flow diagram'.

Exam question (Paper 2: narrative)

Write a story in 120–180 words, beginning with the words:

When I woke up that morning, I knew something was going to happen.

Use the plan from Planning 2.

Improving your work

Checking and polishing

Compare your story with a partner. Go through each other's work, checking for mistakes. Look particularly at the use of past tenses and time linking words. When your story is as good as you can make it, write out a neat copy and give it to your teacher to mark. Keep both the draft copy and the neat copy together in your file.

STUDY TIP 1

You will not have time to write out a neat copy in the exam, but it is useful to do it now so you have something to look back at and revise from later.

Unit 2 Wage slaves

Preview / Planning 1

What is important to you in a job? Choose the five most important factors and arrange them in order of priority.

- ☐ long holidays
- ☐ free lunches
- ☐ high salary
- ☐ flexible working hours
- ☐ job satisfaction
- ☐ some responsibility
- ☐ opportunity for travel

- ☐ having amusing colleagues
- ☐ socially useful
- ☐ normal hours of work
- ☐ long lunch breaks
- ☐ close to home
- ☐ working with other people
- ☐ good career and promotion prospects

Discuss your answers with a partner.

EXAM TIP 3

Number your ideas and organise them in order of priority before you start to write. This is a very simple but effective planning technique.

Selecting relevant information

Look at the information opposite about these four people. Later you will have to choose a job which you think would suit them. Underline the information that might help you make your choice. Compare your answers with a partner.

Alan is 26. He has been unemployed for a long time and is very keen to get a job. He lives in a flat which he shares with a friend. He likes Michael Jackson and Bruce Springsteen. Ideally he would like to do a job that is socially useful, but he is not fussy. He will work any hours. He has a driving licence but not a car.

Betty is 39. She is a single mother with two teenage children and a two-year-old. She gets just enough money to live on but would like to be able to earn a little more. The rest of her family live a long way away. Her children are called Christine, Peter and Emily. The eldest two are at school, but the youngest is still at home. She has a phone but no driving licence.

Charlie is 15 and still at school. He loves football and supports Manchester United. He also reads a lot. He lives with his parents and his grandmother. He wants to earn some extra pocket money before or after school. He is saving up to buy a Walkman.

Doris is a 56-year-old widow. Her husband died two years ago and she has felt very isolated since then. She wants to get out and meet people and she thinks that going back to work would be a good idea. She has her own car and telephone and would like a full-time job.

EXAM TIP 4

It's important to be able to decide which pieces of information are relevant and which can be ignored. This is a very useful skill, especially for the directed writing question.

Giving and justifying opinions

1 Look at the job advertisements below and on page 16. Decide which job would be most suitable for each of the people described above.

When you have decided, compare your answers and the reasons for your choices with a partner.

PART TIME OFFICE ASSISTANT/TYPIST
Required for a friendly expanding and successful Computer Consultancy.
Flexible hours (primarily afternoons).
Salary negotiable.
Please call 031-675-5328
Or send your CV to:
Orion Professional Services Ltd, Orion House, 4 Murrayfield, Edinburgh EH11 4UT.

CHAUFFEURS
FULL & PART TIME
Staff required. Preference will be given to applicants with experience and a good knowledge of Edinburgh.
Minimum age 25.
Tel: 031-225-4616

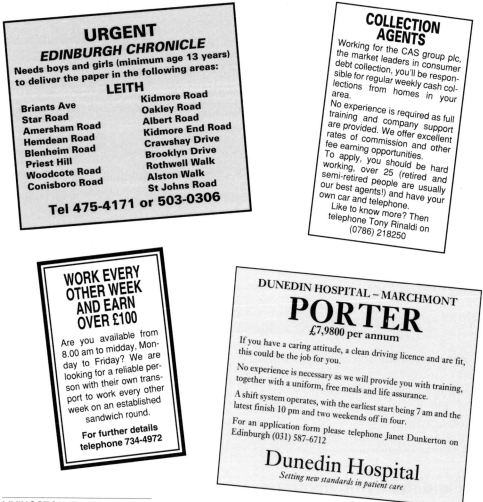
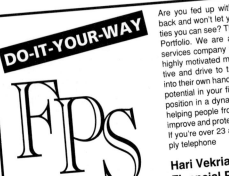

2 Then in your pairs complete the written answer below, using words from the box. You will need to use some words more than once.

since	because	me	so	opinion	furthermore
seems	addition	also	as	feeling	think that

In my .... (1) the most suitable job for Alan would be the porter at the Dunedin Hospital .... (2) it is socially useful. In .... (3), he is prepared to work any hours, which is good .... (4) the hospital operates a shift system. .... (5) he has a driving licence and he does not need any experience.

My .... (6) is .... (7) the best job for Betty would be taking messages from home. She does not want to earn a lot of money and she has to stay at home to look after her youngest child .... (8) this job would suit her very well.

It .... (9) to .... (10) that the best choice for Charlie is delivering papers .... (11) it is the kind of job he can do before or after school. He will be able to earn some extra pocket money, and he is old enough.

I .... (12) that the best job for Doris would be as a collection agent .... (13) it is very suitable for retired and semi-retired people. .... (14) she will get out and meet people and even earn some extra money. She .... (15) has her own car and phone.

3 Now fill in the table below with words and phrases that you can use to give and justify your opinions.

Expressing opinions	*Giving reasons*	*Adding reasons*

EXAM TIP 5

In the directed writing exercise you often have to give an opinion and justify it. Remember the language that you will need!

'I THINK...'
'IN MY OPINION...'

Planning 2

Look at the details of the four people below. Which job advertised on pages 15 and 16 would be most suitable for each of them?

Work in pairs. First underline the important information on the profiles below. Then decide which job you would choose for each person. Make notes of your reasons.

Edward is 46 and only works three days a week at the moment – Monday, Tuesday and Thursday. He does not want to give up this job as he enjoys it. However, he would like to find another part-time job so that he had a little more money. He does not mind what hours he works. He has a car, a phone and his own computer. He loves classical music, and he often goes skating.

Frances is 33 and a mother of three young children – Ann, 7, Rachel, 5, and Jack, 3. Her husband is not very well-paid and she would like to earn some money to pay for extras. Ideally she would like to work a few hours a week in the evenings. Her husband could then look after the children and she would not have to pay for a baby-sitter.

Gillian is 27. She is single and up until now has been working in a bank. She has a flat of her own and a sports car. She is getting bored in her job and would like something much more exciting that will earn her more money. She likes eating out and getting together with her friends for parties.

Harry is 19. He lives with his parents. He has a driving licence and his own car. He recently took a secretarial course, so he can type, take shorthand and he is computer literate. He has not had a job since he left secretarial college three months ago, so he does not mind what he does. He is trying to find a permanent, full-time job, but will settle for less to start with.

Exam question (Paper 3: directed writing)

Write a paragraph (about 50 words) for each person in Planning 2 explaining which job you have chosen for them and why.

"Congratulations, Mr Smith – as soon as I saw you I knew that you were the right man for the job"

Improving your work

Checking and polishing

In pairs, compare your answers. Go through your work together, checking carefully for mistakes. Look particularly at how you have expressed and justified your choices. When your work is as good as you can make it, write out a neat copy if necessary. Keep both the rough draft and the final version of your work together in your file.

Organising your work

Answer the following questions (honestly!):

1 **Do you keep the written work you have done? Yes/No**

If your answer is 'No', perhaps you should think again!
If your answer is 'Yes', then think about these questions:

a) Do you keep it in an organised way?
b) Do you label it with the date you did it, the topic you wrote about, the mark you got for it, etc.?
c) Do you keep the rough notes and plans you used together with the final version?
d) Do you look at both the mistakes and the corrections?
e) Do you ever look at any of it?

2 **Do you collect examples of English writing? Yes/No**

If your answer is 'No', then think about it!
If your answer is 'Yes', then think about these questions:

a) Do you keep examples of different types of writing: formal letters, informal letters, stories, reports, etc.?
b) Do you just push them all in a folder, or do you label them, write notes in the margin, give translations of new words, underline particular phrases, words or structures?
c) Do you ever look at any of them?

3 **Do you keep a notebook or folder with ideas or tips about writing? Yes/No**

If your answer is 'No', then think about whether it should be 'Yes'!
If your answer is 'Yes', then think about these questions:

a) Do you keep a list of useful phrases, such as phrases used in formal letters?
b) Do you keep a list of rules, such as rules for letter layout or rules for using direct speech in narrative?
c) Do you keep a list of words you often forget, misspell or misuse?
d) Do you ever look at any of it?

Work in pairs and discuss which of the ideas given in the questionnaire you think could be useful to you.

Which of the suggestions above would help you to:

- learn from your mistakes
- remember more vocabulary
- learn useful phrases
- write more correctly
- revise more easily

Decide now which ones you are going to try.

STUDY TIP 2

Get into the habit of organising your work. This will help you write better, improve faster and remember more easily what you have learnt.

Unit 3 On the road

Preview

Are you a good traveller?

Choose a, b or c for each of the questions below.
Then add up your score and see if you are a good traveller or not.

1 *While you are abroad someone steals your money, passport and tickets. What do you do first?*
  a Sit down and cry.
  b Go to the police.
  c Go to your Embassy.

2 *Your flight is delayed for 24 hours. What do you do?*
  a Wait in the airport until your flight eventually leaves.
  b Go to the airline and ask what they intend to do.
  c Check into a hotel for the night.

'Ladies and gentlemen, please don't panic …'

3 *You are in a café abroad. Someone invites you to try a local speciality dish. What do you do?*
  a Refuse.
  b Accept and have a second helping.
  c Taste one spoonful and make excuses.

4 *You have a 24-hour stopover in New York. What do you do?*
  a Check into the Hilton, have a meal, a bath and a sleep.
  b Go sightseeing and visit some places you haven't yet seen.
  c Meet up with a friend who is there on a business trip.

Score 3 points for each b, 1 point for each c, and 0 points for each a.
10 and over: Excellent – you are an experienced and adventurous traveller.
6–9: Not too bad, but you obviously don't travel very often.
0–5: Poor – a real stay-at-home. You must get out more often.

Planning 1

Work in pairs. Imagine you are going to travel through Africa together on holiday. A friend of yours is an expert on Africa. Write down the questions that you would like to ask him or her before you go.

Think about topics such as health, climate, bureaucracy, etc.

Giving advice

1 Put the prompts into the correct column in the box below.

Why don't you . . . ?   If I were you, I'd . . .
You'd better . . .   It might be a good idea to . . .
You really should . . .   Why not . . . ?
You ought to . . .

Suggestions	*Strong advice*

2 What advice do you think your friend gave you in answer to your questions in Planning 1 above? Make sentences from the prompts above and the pictures below.

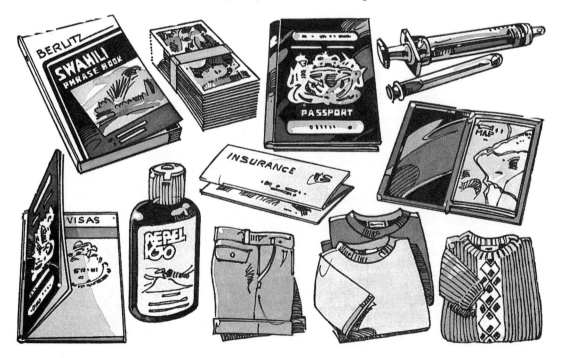

EXAM TIP 6

Think about what your reader
wants to know. Making a list of
questions is often a useful way of
collecting ideas before you start any
writing task.

Punctuating correctly

1 Complete the table below by putting in the correct name for each feature of punctuation,
and then using a coloured pen, correctly punctuate the sentences on the right.

Feature	Name	Use	Example
A B C	....	to start sentences	we need a visa to go there.
		for names	tunisia and algeria
		with 'I'	Tomorrow i leave for Egypt.
.	....	to end sentences	Travelling by train is cheap
,	....	to separate items in a list (but not before 'and')	cholera malaria polio and typhoid
		to add information	You must see the River Nile which flows through Egypt.
:	....	to start a list	Take a mixture of currency £ sterling, French francs and US dollars.
		to add an explanation	Avoid drinking unboiled water it is a major source of disease.
;	....	to separate items in lists of phrases	So remember what you need: lots of money the right vaccinations the right visas.
'	....	to show letters left out	Youll need a vaccination certificate.
		to indicate possession	The travellers main problem is time.

2 Now rewrite the passage below putting in the correct punctuation.

you should take clothes for hot and cold climates the desert even though its in africa gets very cold at night in addition dont forget the small essentials water purifying tablets a needle and cotton a pair of sunglasses and one or two good books i also take a penknife a sleeping bag and a stove

---

EXAM TIP 7

Correct punctuation is important. Allow some time specially to check your punctuation when you have finished writing.

Planning 2

Work in pairs. A penfriend from another country is coming to stay with you. Make a list of the questions you think they will want to ask before they arrive.

Look at the layout of the informal letters below. Are the following statements *true* or *false*?

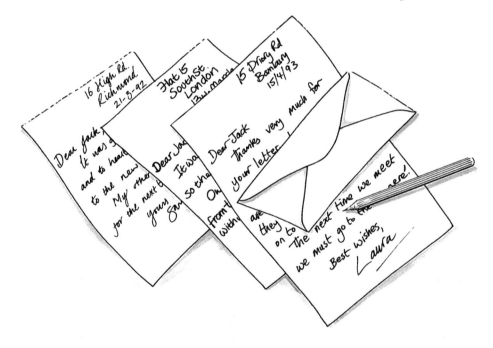

1 You must not divide the letter into paragraphs.
2 You begin 'Dear . . . ' and use the forename of the person you are writing to.
3 You need not put the date.
4 You must put the full address and postcode.
5 You can finish 'Best wishes' or 'Yours'.
6 You sign the letter with your full name.

Exam question (Paper 2: informal letter)

A penfriend from Canada is coming to stay with you for three weeks. Write a letter to them giving advice about any arrangements they need to make before they come, and what they need to bring with them. (120–180 words)

Improving your work

Checking and polishing

Compare your letter with a partner. Go through each other's work. Check for mistakes – look particularly at the expressions of advice and the punctuation. Has your partner left out any good advice? Have they got any good advice that you missed? When your letter is as good as possible, write out a neat copy. Keep both the draft copy and the neat copy together in your file.

Self-assessment 1

Look back at the mistakes you have made in your last three compositions. How do you feel about the standard of your writing? Add to the list given in the table below and tick the appropriate boxes.

	Good	Okay	Poor
Organisation of ideas			
Spelling			
Tenses			
Grammar			
Punctuation			
Vocabulary			
Others			

Which areas need extra work? Your teacher will suggest ways you can improve your weakest areas.

STUDY TIP 3

Work out which mistakes you make most often and concentrate on getting rid of them. Draw up a chart of what you need to improve, and how you could practise. Cross items off when you feel you have improved them.

Unit 4   A tall, dark, handsome stranger

Planning technique:	using a 'spidergraph'
Language skills:	adjectives for describing people; ordering adjectives
Exam question:	paper 2: description
Improving:	adding interest and personalisation

Preview

Work in pairs. Look at the people in the photos below and discuss them. Can you guess their ages, nationalities, and jobs? What sort of people do you think they are? Decide on their characters, their likes and dislikes, and their hobbies.

When you have decided, compare your answers with another pair.

Planning 1

The diagram below is sometimes called a 'spidergraph' or 'mind map'. It helps you to plan out your ideas before you start to write.

In pairs complete the diagram using the words in the box underneath it.

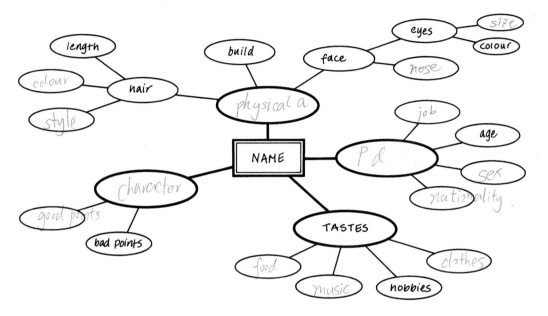

personal details	food	music	colour	size	clothes	job	sex
physical appearance		character	style	nose	nationality		good points

A 'spidergraph' or 'mind map' is a useful way of grouping information. It also helps to plan paragraphs.

Adjectives for describing people

1 The words below can all be used to describe people. Work in pairs and put the words into three or more groups. Each pair should decide for themselves how to group the words.

friendly	slim	stubborn	dark	plump	short	independent
handsome	tall	shy	scruffy	smart	fair	attractive	curly
honest	wavy	thin	blond	generous		

Compare your grouping with that of other pairs.

2 Which (if any) of the words in the lists could be used in a negative or critical way when describing a person?

3 Using the box below, make sentences about the people in the Preview exercise. Then make up some more sentences of your own.

He		–	a film star
	looks		attractive
		like	he's had a bad day
		as if	she's friendly
She			honest
			a boxer
			....
			....
			(*add your own suggestions*)

Ordering adjectives

If there is more than one adjective in front of a noun, it is important to get them in the right order. The order depends on the type of adjective.

1 First match each type of adjective to its example:

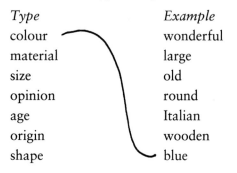

Type	*Example*
colour	wonderful
material	large
size	old
opinion	round
age	Italian
origin	wooden
shape	blue

2 Now look at the phrases below, work out the order for different types of adjectives in English and complete the table.

- a beautiful Chinese silk blouse
- a small red Italian shirt
- a horrible wide yellow tie
- a large old black hat
- a round pink face
- a large square cotton handkerchief

Order of adjectives

1..   5..

2..   6..

3..   7..

4. *Shape* ....

3 Now rewrite the phrases below putting the adjectives in the correct order.

a) a(n) blue/stylish/Armani jacket
b) a leather/fashionable/short skirt
c) brown/attractive/short hair
d) a(n) red/ugly/large nose
e) small/leather/black shoes
f) blue/large/round eyes

NICK DOWNES

Planning 2

Draw a 'spidergraph' for someone you know well – a good friend or a member of your family. Fill in as much detail as possible.

When you have finished, compare your work with that of other people in your class.

Exam question (Paper 2: description)

One of your friends is going to Australia. Your Australian penfriend has invited them to stay for a few days. Write to your penfriend accepting the invitation and giving a description of your friend. (120–180 words)

Improving your work

Checking and polishing

Compare your description with a partner. Go through each other's work. Check for mistakes. Look at the use and order of adjectives. Can you improve your partner's or your own description? When your description is as good as possible, write out a neat copy. Keep your 'spidergraph' plan, your draft copy and your neat copy together in your file.

Adding interest and personalisation

1 Work in pairs. Look at the exam question below. Which of the following extracts from the exam answers is better? Why?

Write a letter to your English-speaking penfriend, describing yourself. Tell your penfriend about your family, job, hobbies, etc.

1   My brother and I get on particularly well. He's older than me, but not too bossy! He's amusing and also adventurous. We often go climbing or sailing together. It's exciting and sometimes dangerous, but he's very responsible too, so I feel safe with him.

2   I've got one sister. She's older than me. She is a nurse. She's tall and slim. She's got nice brown hair. We go out together to lots of different places. We have a nice time. Sometimes we go on holiday together.

Which of the following make the extract interesting?

– It uses longer words.
– It uses a wider variety of adjectives.
– It has longer sentences.
– It gives details.
– It gives general information.
– It is more personal – tells you what the writer thinks.
– It is longer.

2 Rewrite this passage in a more interesting way.

I've got one brother. He's quite young. He's nice looking and quite tall. He's got lots of hobbies. He has a good job. He earns lots of money. Some people fight with their brothers and sisters.

EXAM TIP 9

Try to make your answer as interesting as possible. Use a wide variety of adjectives and try to link your ideas together in longer sentences. Give details where you can rather than just vague information. Add your opinion – this makes the text more personal and automatically more interesting.

Unit 5 **Through the grapevine**

Planning technique:	listing advantages and disadvantages
Language skills:	paragraphing; talking about advantages and disadvantages
Exam question:	paper 2: discussion essay
Improving:	what we write

Preview

Find someone in your class who, in their own country:

– reads a newspaper every day   ....

– doesn't have a television in their home   ....

– never listens to the radio   ....

– thinks they watch too much television   ....

– has had their picture in a newspaper   ....

Planning 1

Work in pairs. Make a list of the advantages and disadvantages of pocket televisions.

Advantages	Disadvantages

EXAM TIP 10

This technique is very useful for planning discussion essays. It is especially useful if you have to discuss two sides of an argument.

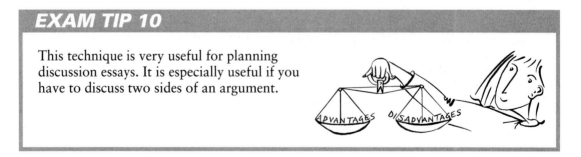

32

Paragraphing

'An increase in the number of pocket televisions will not benefit society.'
What do you think?

Work in pairs. Look at the answer to this question below. The paragraphs have been mixed up. Read the four paragraphs and put them in the right order. Write the correct letter in the table below.

A There are, however, some advantages. The pocket TV is very convenient. We can take it anywhere and never miss an important programme. Another good thing is that sports enthusiasts can watch important events wherever they wish. And one further benefit is the TV information services. These will be available at any time.

B Twenty years ago Walkmans did not exist. Now everyone has them. Will the pocket television, one of the latest inventions, be as popular in 20 years' time?

C In my opinion the most important factor is its convenience. This will benefit society as long as we do not let it take over our lives.

D One major drawback of the pocket television is the tiny screen. It is so small that it may damage people's eyes. Another problem is that it is so convenient. People may watch one in meetings or at parties, perhaps even while driving. This is not acceptable and could be dangerous. A further disadvantage is that people may watch TV even more than they do now.

	Letter	*Heading*
Para 1	....	....
Para 2	....	....
Para 3	....	....
Para 4	....	....

Now give each paragraph a heading from the box below.

opinion   advantages   introduction   disadvantages

Check your answers with another pair.

EXAM TIP 11

This paragraph order is a good way of structuring a discussion essay. A similar structure can be used with the 'opinion' type of discussion essay – see Unit 9.

The important thing to remember is that there is a clear beginning and a

Talking about advantages and disadvantages

Look through the composition in Paragraphing on page 33 and write in the box below all the phrases used to introduce advantages and disadvantages.

A major	advantage	
....	....	
....	....	is . . .
One further	problem	
....	....	
....	....	

Now work in small groups or pairs and use these expressions to talk about the advantages and disadvantages of the following:

– having a telephone
– having a fax machine
– being famous
– allowing free copying of
  audio and video cassettes

linden.

Planning 2

Using the technique practised in Planning 1, list the advantages and disadvantages of censorship. Also list ideas for your introduction and conclusion.

Introduction	Advantages	Disadvantages	Conclusion

When you have finished your lists, compare them with one or two other people in your class. Add to your list any good ideas that you have missed, and give them any good ideas that they have missed.

Exam question (Paper 2: discussion essay)

'We are nearly in the 21st century. We have no need for censorship'.

What do you think? (120–180 words)

Improving your work

Checking and polishing

Compare your composition with a partner. Go through each other's work. Check for mistakes – look particularly at the paragraphing and the expressions used to talk about advantages and disadvantages. When your composition is as good as possible, write out a neat copy. Keep both the draft copy and the neat copy together in your file.

What we write

What do you write? Tick the appropriate boxes in the table below, and add as many things to the list as you can.

	in your own language	*in English*
notes		
messages		
letters to friends		
business letters		
letters of complaint		
descriptions		
formal compositions		
narratives (stories)		
....		
....		

Which of these are for your own personal use, and which are intended to be read by other people?

What types of writing do you need for the Cambridge First Certificate exam?

Unit 6 **Being green**

Planning technique: using a questionnaire
Language skills: evaluating information; linking words for reasons and results
Exam question: paper 3: directed writing
Improving: why we write

Preview

Rearrange the letters below to form words. Then write the words in the correct column in the table below.

rpeload	ehawl	eonhricros
sag	yiierelcttc	eaunclr owrep
seeabttri	lasgs	perap
idwn	ocla	luuniamim
arillgo	ytrse	adapn

Sources of power	Things that can be recycled	Endangered animals

'Have you got an
endangered species export licence?'

36

Planning 1

Look at the questionnaire. Complete it by adding some sentences of your own. Then fill in your opinion by ticking the appropriate column. Finally get together with a partner and fill in his/her opinion.

Use phrases from the box below where appropriate.

Agreeing	*Disagreeing*
Absolutely.	Yes, but . . .
Exactly.	Don't you think . . . ?
I (quite) agree.	I'm not sure I quite agree there.
That's exactly what I think.	I'm afraid I don't quite agree there.
I couldn't agree with you more.	

	You		Partner		
	agree	disagree	agree	disagree	
Animals Animals should not be used to test cosmetics. We should do everything necessary to avoid the extinction of any species of animal.					
Pollution Nuclear power is the 'cleanest' form of power. The nuclear programme must be developed further.					
Natural Resources Widespread deforestation must be stopped.					
Food					

One of the biggest problems with writing can be having enough ideas. Try to think of as many ideas as you can by asking yourself questions about the topic.

'WHAT WOULD.... THINK?'

'WHAT DO I FEEL ABOUT...?'

'DO I AGREE WITH....?'

Evaluating information

Darlingham Council, Darlingham, New South Wales has underspent its budget by £20,000. They are trying to decide what to do with the extra money.

There are four plans:
– plant a forest
– increase public transport services
– improve recycling facilities
– send the money to Hungerlink – a Third World charity

Read the information and do the exercise on page 40.

PLANT A TREE – PLANT A TREE

The environment is the major concern of our age. Many people feel they would like to do something to improve it.

PLANT A TREE – PLANT A TREE

Almost a third of our natural forest cover has disappeared over the last 8,000 years. This has destroyed rare flora and fauna.

PLANT A TREE – PLANT A TREE

Planting trees not only helps restore the balance of nature but also creates a more pleasant environment in which to live.

PLANT A TREE – PLANT A TREE

PLANT A TREE – PLANT A TREE

Forest destruction alters the climate by reducing the amount of water circulating between the trees and clouds, thus increasing the level of CO_2 in the atmosphere.

PLANT A TREE – PLANT A TREE

Forest destruction is responsible for about half the extra CO_2 added to the atmosphere in the last two centuries.

PLANT A TREE – PLANT A TREE

For £20 you could plant a tree; for £200 an orchard; for £20,000 a forest.

PLANT A TREE – PLANT A TREE

DARLINGHAM COUNCIL

13/5/92

MEMO

To: all councillors
From: Ray Grant, Environmental Officer

There are two areas where the Council has not yet done what it promised at the last election.

1 Transport
We promised that we would increase the public transport services both inside and outside the town. There would be better bus and train connections to neighbouring towns; and more bus routes and more frequent services within the town. This was to encourage motorists to use public transport rather than their own cars, and thus reduce traffic pollution.

2 Recycling
We promised a campaign to improve recycling facilities for paper, glass and aluminium, and to advertise these services more widely. We also promised to introduce recycling facilities for other materials, if possible. An increase in recycling will help save resources.

We have not yet done anything to carry out these promises. I feel we should take action on one or, if possible, both these policies as soon as possible.

Evaluate the four possibilities above by deciding which plan is the best and which the second best from the different points of view in the left-hand column of the table below. Put *P* (Plant a tree), *T* (Transport), *R* (Recycling) or *H* (Hungerlink) in one of the right-hand columns according to what you think. For example if you think planting a tree is the best plan from the point of view of the effect on local pollution, put a *P* in the best plan column.

	Best plan	*Second best plan*
effect on local pollution		
effect on local people		
effect on council's political status		
easy to carry out		
usefulness		
effect on local environment		
benefit to the most people		
long-term benefit		
popularity with local people		

Which plan do you think is the best overall? Which is the worst?

Now compare your answers in pairs and small groups. Give reasons for your choices.

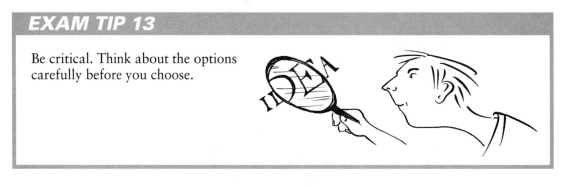

EXAM TIP 13

Be critical. Think about the options carefully before you choose.

Linking words for reasons and results

1 Look at these paragraphs about two of the plans above. Underline the words used to show reasons and results (e.g. since, as a result etc.).

> I think Darlingham Council should send the money to Hungerlink because more people will benefit this way. It is also a good idea as it is easy to do. It does not benefit local people at all and as a result it may not be popular. However, the money will be helping people who really need it, so it might not be too politically damaging.

The council could also improve local transport since pollution of the atmosphere is a very serious problem. They could provide enough public transport so that people would not need to use their own cars. This would cut down air pollution and traffic noise, and greatly improve the local environment. It would, therefore, be a popular choice. In addition, they had promised to do this, so it would be politically useful.

2 Now complete the two paragraphs below using some of the linking words you have underlined in the passages above.

The council should not spend the money on recycling .... (1) this is not the best option. There are already some recycling facilities .... (2) it would not have a great effect. Most people think pollution is a much more important problem than recycling at the moment and .... (3) this would not be a very popular plan.

The council should not spend the money on planting a forest .... (4) this would be a waste of money. It would not benefit many people at all and would, ... (5), be very unpopular. In addition the forest would probably be planted outside the town. .... (6) it would not benefit the local environment very much.

3 Now read through all four paragraphs, and say whether you agree or disagree with them, giving reasons.

"This is Mr Trimp from the Town and Country Planning Department. He's here to demonstrate the proposals for the old town"

Planning 2

Surprisingly perhaps, Darlingham Council decided to plant a forest.

Look at the map on the next page, read the information which follows it, and decide where you think the forest should be planted and why.

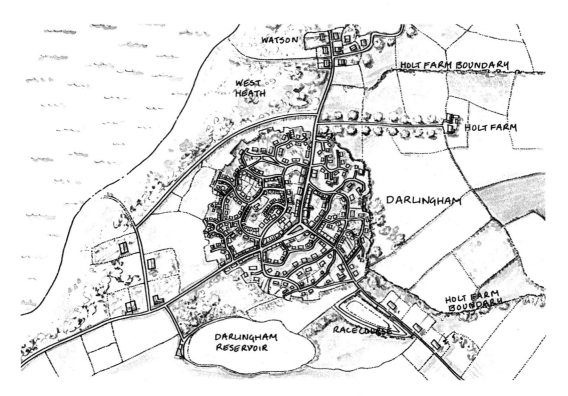

Holt Farm
Darlingham
3/6/92

Dear Sir or Madam,

I object most strongly to the suggestion that Darlingham Council should plant trees on Holt Farm property.

My family and I have lived and worked here for over a hundred years. We have provided food and jobs for the local community, and contributed much to the life of the town of Darlingham.

You cannot repay us like this.

Eric Holt

Eric Holt

MEMO

Darlingham Racecourse

To: Press Officer
From: Chief Steward
Date: 2/6/92

I have just been informed that the Council are considering getting rid of the racecourse and using it as the site for this forest they want to plant.

Please organise a campaign to stop this. Point out how popular horse racing is, how much money we bring into the town during race weekends, and how it is the one activity that makes Milton famous.

I suggest a notice to all the papers, and letters to all the Councillors.

Threat to West Heath Industrial Site

Local councillor, Edward Abbott, today confirmed the possibility that the new business park at West Heath, which would be the site of six factories and a possible 500 jobs for local people, might not now happen.

'We know that the business park is important for the local employment and economy', he said. 'However, our environmental policy is also important.' He stressed that no decision had yet been reached and that the councillors were listening to opinions from everyone in the community.

Discuss your answers in pairs.

Exam question (Paper 3: directed writing)

Read the information in Planning 2 again. Darlingham Council is considering three different places to plant a forest. Where are the three places?

1 ....

....

2 ....

....

3 ....

....

→

Which do you think is the best place and why? (50 words)

....

....

....

....

....

Which do you think is the worst place and why? (50 words)

....

....

....

....

....

Improving your work

Checking and polishing

Compare your answer with a partner. Go through each other's work. Check for mistakes –
look particularly at the reasons you have given for your answers and the way you have
expressed those reasons.

Why we write

Why do you write? Tick the appropriate boxes
in the table and add to the list.

to give information	
to make a complaint	
to apply for a job	
to describe someone	
to pass an exam	
....	
....	

EXAM TIP 14

Remember why you are writing. It will
affect what you write and how you write
it. A social letter to a friend will be
different from one to a friend apologising
for forgetting a dinner invitation.

WHY AM
I WRITING?

Unit 7 **Learn a language**

Planning technique:	'brainstorming'
Language skills:	letter-writing rules; making requests
Exam question:	paper 2: formal letter
Improving:	clear handwriting

Preview / Planning 1

'Brainstorming'

Work in pairs. You are going to spend four weeks in the summer at a language school in Edinburgh in Scotland. Write down as many ideas, words and phrases as you can in each column below. Do not write sentences – notes are okay. Do not worry about any mistakes. Concentrate on getting as many ideas as possible. You have five minutes.

What you want to know about Edinburgh	*What you want to know about the school*	*What you will take with you*

Compare your ideas with another pair.

EXAM TIP 15

'Brainstorming' is often a useful way to start planning a composition. Just write down everything you think of. Don't worry about mistakes yet.

45

Letter-writing rules

Laying out a letter

Helsinki
3/2/93

Dear Morag,

Thank you very much for your invitation to stay with you during the summer so that I can go to a language school in Edinburgh. I'd love to come and I'm really looking forward to it already. The dates that suit me best would be from about 1st to 24th July. How is that for you?

Will you give me an idea what sort of clothes to bring? I imagine the climate is probably rather like Finland in the summer — some rain, some sun. And can you tell me what there is to do outside Edinburgh and how easy it is to travel around in Scotland. I've never been before and I want to make the most of it.

Do you think you could also find out a bit about the language schools there? I'll write off for all the brochures but it's not the same as having local knowledge. I'd really appreciate it if you could find out which are the best and which to avoid.

Thanks very much again. Can't wait till July.

Best wishes
Marja-Liisa

Upplandsgatan 2 II
214 70 Malmö
Sweden

The Principal
The Scottish Language Centre   3rd February 1993
Princes St
Edinburgh

Dear Sir or Madam

I am thinking of coming to Edinburgh next July for one month to learn English.

Please could you send me details of your classes, any special courses you offer and how much you charge.

I would also be grateful if you could send me information about accommodation. Does the Centre have its own accommodation service or will I have to find somewhere to stay myself?

Finally I would appreciate it if you could let me have details of any exams I would be able to take at this time.

I look forward to hearing from you.

Yours faithfully,

Eva Petersson

Eva Petersson (Ms)

Work in pairs. Look at the letters opposite. Which is formal and which informal? Study the layout of the letters and tick the correct column(s) in the table below. The first one has been done for you.

	Informal letters	*Formal letters*	*Neither*
You usually begin **Dear . . .**	✓	✓	
You put your name in the top right-hand corner.			
You put your address in the top right-hand corner.			
You need not put your full address.			
You should put the date under your address.			
You write the name and address of the person you are writing to in the top left-hand corner.			
You do not put paragraphs.			
You can finish **Yours sincerely / Yours faithfully.**			
You always use the first name of the person you are writing to.			
You can sign your full name.			
You can finish **Best wishes / Love from.**			
You should put your name under your signature.			
You can use contractions (e.g. **I'd, I'll**).			

EXAM TIP 16

Lay your letters out correctly. It's not particularly difficult and is something you can guarantee you'll get right in an exam if you know it well.

Starting and finishing a letter

Fill in the table with words and phrases from the boxes below:

	Starting	*Finishing*
Intimate		→
Family		→ *Love from*
Friendly		→
Formal I		→
Formal II	*Dear Sir or Madam*	→

Dear Alice
Dear Uncle Jim
Dear Sir or Madam
Darling
Dear Mrs Cooper

Yours faithfully
Lots of love and kisses
Love from
Yours sincerely
Best wishes

Making requests

1 Look at the two letters in Planning 1 and write the expressions used to make requests in the table below.

Friendly	*Polite*	*Formal*

Compare your answer with a partner and together add any other ways you know of making requests.

2 How do you decide whether to use a friendly, a polite or a formal request?

3 Work in pairs or small groups. How would you write these requests to (a) your best friend and (b) an elderly relative you don't know very well?

- You are going on holiday for three weeks and you write asking if they will visit your flat a couple of times a week to feed your goldfish.
- You write asking if you can call round next weekend to collect a book they offered to lend you.
- You write asking if they could send you the address of a mutual friend.
- Your car has been totally destroyed in an accident and you write asking to borrow enough money to buy a new car.
- You write asking if they will guarantee a bank loan for you.

Planning 2

Look at the exam question below. Write down as many ideas, and useful words and phrases as you can in five minutes. Do not worry about the accuracy of what you write.

When you have done that, compare what you have written with a partner. Add any good ideas of theirs and give them any good ideas of yours.

Then organise your ideas into a sensible plan for the letter.

'Do you know another word for thesaurus?'

Exam question (Paper 2: formal letter)

You want to go to university in Canada. Write to the University of Quebec asking for information. You will need to find out about courses, costs, accommodation and how good your English needs to be. (120–180 words)

Improving your work

Checking and polishing

Compare your answer with a partner. Go through each other's work. Check for mistakes – look particularly at the layout of the letter and the language used to make requests. When your composition is as good as possible, write out a neat copy. Keep your original plan, the draft copy and the neat copy together in your file.

Clear handwriting

Look at these students' writing and answer the questions opposite.

My best friend is Stephane. It's my neighbour in France but he is Italian. He is as tall as mine, he has Dark hair and eyes and a good looking. He likes beautiful cars and nice women like all Italian people. The most important I think that he understands me before than I speak and he knows what I think in my head — It's the same for me. He is intelligent and generous.

I'd like to speak about my best friend. Her name is Renee Catherine & Amissah she's 21 year old she's studying law In Paris, she's very Thin and told She has a hair cut and a brown eyes she's very kind and clever she likes speaking and likes Animals, and likes driving a car, it's her favourite hobby.

His Name is Maker.
He is tall and ~~smitt~~ slim. he has a Black hair and brown eyes. he has a big body.
He is a good friend, and ~~He~~ he always ~~do for helping~~ helps his friends on something else.
He wants to ~~studying~~ study in the university, but he hasn't ~~a~~ any money. So he works very hard ~~for~~ to get money.

My best friend name is Anxantonic. We were together in the same school. We knew each other 13 years ago. After that we changed ~~the~~ schools, she (~~choosed~~ chose) a different school to ~~tite~~ me, but we continue the relasion even now. She ~~has~~ has braw'd hair, blue eyes. She is not very tall and she (curly) has frecclles.

Howard is a teacher of ARABIC language. He is a queiet person. Although he is ~~Althogh Althogt~~ very nice and friandly He alÈways likes to be in farm with animal ~~Hexe~~ looks abit fat strang. He has a black eyes and black hair

1 Which handwriting is the easiest to read? Why?
2 Which is the most difficult to read? Why?
3 Which student has corrected their work most carefully? How?

Look back at your work over the last few units. How would you grade it on the scale below?

(VERY NEAT AND EASY TO READ)   0 .... 1 .... 2 .... 3 .... 4 5   (UNTIDY AND DIFFICULT TO READ)

Ask other people to grade your handwriting. Do you agree with them?

EXAM TIP 17

Make your writing legible and your corrections tidy.

REMEMBER!
* The examiners can only give marks for what they can actually read! Don't forget they have several hundred scripts to mark.
* If your work is tidy and clear, the examiner is more likely to think well of you!
* If your work is untidy, the examiner may think you have not put much effort into it – even if this is not true!
* It is more difficult for examiners to follow what you are saying in your answer if it is difficult to read.

Unit 8 Bestsellers

Planning technique: selecting relevant information
Language skills: characteristics of spoken language; expressing attitude
Exam question: paper 2: speech
Improving: using resources

Preview

Write down the titles and authors of three books that have greatly impressed you.

Work in pairs or small groups. Compare your choices and explain why you chose what you did.

Planning 1

You have to explain to your class why you liked a particular book. Look at the list of points below and cross out those that you think would not be relevant in such a situation.

- The characters are very real.
- The author understands the criminal mind well.
- The book is 224 pages long.
- The plot is clever and original.
- I found it easy to identify with the main character.
- My sister likes reading too.
- The ending is exciting.
- The picture on the cover is striking.
- The story is set in Arizona.
- The descriptions are vivid.
- The blurb on the back is interesting.
- The book paints a fascinating picture of life in the depression.
- My friend Sue liked it.
- It conveys a powerful socialist message.
- The author had written three books before this one.
- The author uses language in a simple yet effective way.
- The author pays great attention to historical accuracy.
- I've never been to Arizona.

Compare your answers with a partner. Are there any points you disagree about? Discuss any differences.

EXAM TIP 18

You don't have to use all your ideas
when you plan a composition. Choose
the most relevant and important ideas
you have noted down.

Characteristics of spoken language

1 Look at each pair of sentences below and decide which is more likely to be spoken
English. In each case underline the words that help you decide.

1 a) She's written quite a few other similar books, I mean about witches and stuff like
that.

   b) She has written a number of other books on the supernatural.

2 a) Now just a few words about the author, who, as I was saying, died earlier this year
in Cannes.

   b) The author, Charles Keene, died earlier this year in Cannes.

3 a) In the opening chapters we learn about Thelma's life at home with her stepfather.

   b) At the beginning he looks at what Thelma's life is like and how she gets on with her
stepfather.

4 a) Professor Hackett then decides to leave Los Angeles and take up a new post in
Chicago.

   b) And then after that the Professor decides he's had enough of Los Angeles so he
finds a new job in Chicago.

5 a) Well, to begin with it seems as if the detective has sorted everything, but the
author's got one or two surprises up her sleeve.

   b) The case appears to be solved in the first few chapters. However, not everything is
quite as it seems.

2 Now look back at the sentences on page 53 and decide which of the features below are characteristics of spoken language. Cross out those which do not apply to spoken language.

- no contractions
- more passives
- more phrasal verbs
- more formal words and phrases
- more fillers (you see, etc.)
- more slang words and expressions
- avoids phrasal verbs
- contractions
- prefers active verbs

EXAM TIP 19

When you write a speech, try to make it sound like natural spoken English. Imagine someone speaking.

Expressing attitude

Work in pairs. Complete the table below. Use your dictionaries if necessary.

Verb	Adjective
amuse	amusing
impress	....
....	interesting
....	exciting
thrill	....
....	boring
convince	....
delight	....
....	fascinating
offend	....
depress	....
annoy	....
....	irritating

Look at these opinions:

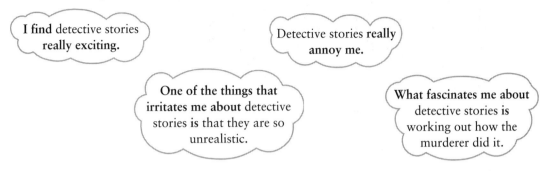

I find detective stories really exciting.

Detective stories really annoy me.

One of the things that irritates me about detective stories is that they are so unrealistic.

What fascinates me about detective stories is working out how the murderer did it.

Work in small groups. Choose six of the following types of books. Use some of the words from the table above and tell each other what you think.

romantic stories   westerns   detective stories   cookery books
science fiction books   novels   biographies   travel books   thrillers
comic books   grammar books   this book

Planning 2

1 Choose one of the books you talked about in the Preview exercise and make a list of points about why you like this book. Try and think of six to eight different reasons.

2 Exchange lists with a partner. Read your partner's list and decide if all the points on their list are relevant. If you think some of them are not, discuss them.

Exam question (Paper 2: speech)

Your teacher has asked everyone in the class to give a speech recommending one of their favourite books to their classmates. Write the speech that you would give. If you want to you can write about one of the set books. (120–180 words)

Improving your work

Checking and polishing

Compare your answer with a partner. Go through each other's work. Check for mistakes – look particularly at the use of spoken language and how they have expressed their attitudes. When your composition is as good as possible, write out a neat copy. Keep your draft and the neat copy together in your file.

Using resources

1 Which of the following resources are available to you (in school or outside)?

English–English dictionary
bilingual dictionary
coursebook
English-language radio and TV programmes
English-language films at the cinema
English-language books, magazines, etc.
English speakers to talk to

2 Can you think of any other resources?

Make enquiries to find out whether you can find other resources you think might be 'unavailable', for example:

- Ask local newsagents' shops and bookshops if they could order English-language items for you.
- If your school has a library, ask if they could get more English-language books.
- Ask at the local library for information about English clubs.
- Ask your teacher for information about getting an English-speaking penpal.
- Ask your teacher or bookshop to recommend good coursebooks or grammar reference books.
- Ask other students in your school if they could lend you English-language books.
- Ask family or friends who travel abroad to bring back English-language newspapers, leaflets, etc. for you.

Make a written note of things such as the times of English-language radio and TV programmes, the addresses of English-language clubs, penpal organisations, etc.

STUDY TIP 4

There are probably more resources around than you realise. Find out about them. Use them.

Unit 9 **Family life**

Preview

Work in pairs. Fill in the speech and thought bubbles in the cartoons below. Compare your answers with another pair.

Planning 1

You have been given this title for a composition:

'Looking after old people should be the responsibility of the family'. Discuss.

Work in pairs and plan your composition by adding notes to the diagram below.

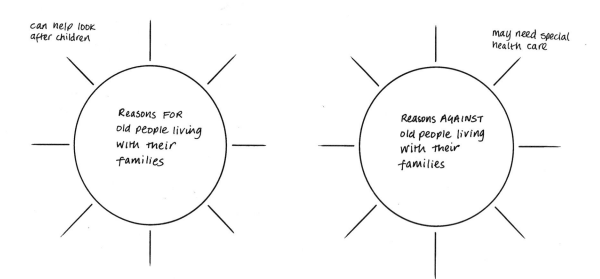

can help look
after children

Reasons FOR
old people living
with their
families

may need special
health care

Reasons AGAINST
old people living
with their
families

EXAM TIP 20

'Headlights' are a useful way of planning a
discussion essay. They help you to collect
your thoughts.

*"I blame all my problems on coming from
a broken egg"*

Opening and closing paragraphs

1 Look at the four paragraphs below. Which would be the best opening for the
composition in Planning 1 above? What is wrong with the others?

A My next door neighbour is 73 years old and she lives on her own. Her son lives quite nearby.
  He comes round twice a week to check on her.

B Throughout this century it has become more and more common in the western world for old
  people to live on their own or in old people's homes rather than with their families. People
  from other cultures often find this practice barbaric, but are they right?

C Of course old people should be looked after by their families – after all they looked after their
  children when they were young.

D In some ways it is a good idea for old people to live with their families, and in some ways it is
  not. Some people might be very happy to have their old relatives living with them. Some old
  people might not want to live with their family.

2 Now look at these four paragraphs. Which would be the best closing paragraph for the
composition? What is wrong with the others?

A In my country we do not have the terrible situation of old people living in hospital because
  they have nowhere else to go. Furthermore, because we look after old people in the family,
  there are very few old people's homes.

B They have great knowledge and experience which they can pass on. If they have a pension
  they can help financially. And of course they can help with the babysitting and housework and
  so on.

C As you can see this is a difficult matter. It is both a moral and a practical problem. My feeling
  is that each family should consider all the arguments carefully and decide what best suits
  them.

D I will never live with my family when I grow old. My cousin's parents lived with him and they
  both survived into their nineties. He never had any independence at all.

3 Now cross out the items below which are not true.

An opening paragraph should:

– give examples
– give your opinion
– show there are two sides to the question
– make a general comment on the subject
– talk about what the question means
– talk about someone you know who is relevant to the question

A closing paragraph should:

– add some extra points of interest and information
– summarise the arguments very briefly in one or two sentences
– add extra arguments to support your opinion
– state your own opinion
– give examples to support your opinion
– state any conclusions you reach

4 Now work with a partner. Look at the exam question opposite and work out a good opening and a good closing paragraph.

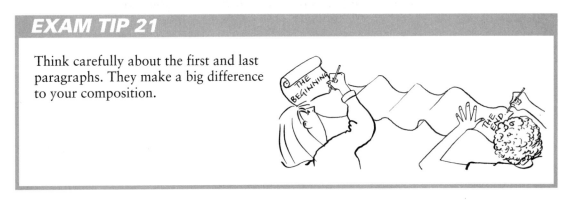

EXAM TIP 21

Think carefully about the first and last paragraphs. They make a big difference to your composition.

Recognising how a text links together

Look at the text below, which was written in answer to the question in Planning 1. Mark the text to show how some words are used to refer backwards and forwards. The first few have been done for you.

Throughout this century it has become more and more common in the western world for old people to live on their own or in old people's homes rather than with their families. People from other cultures often find this practice barbaric; but are they right?

There are many reasons why it is a good idea for grandparents to live with their families. It stresses that families are important and teaches the grandchildren a proper respect for the elderly. The grandparents are able to help the parents with the benefit of their knowledge and experience; and to give practical assistance with things like housework, baby-sitting, and so on. There is also the moral argument that the grandparents looked after the parents when they were children so now it is time for them to repay the debt.

There are, however, reasons why it is not such a good idea. People do not always get on very well with their parents-in-law and if the grandparents try to interfere in the life of the family too much it could cause serious problems. Furthermore when the grandparents become very old and frail, it may take a lot of time to look after them. This sort of care is best provided by experts in an old people's home.

Planning 2

Look at the exam question. Use the techniques you practised in Planning 1 to plan your composition. Use the opening and closing paragraphs you worked out in exercise 4 above.

When you have finished, compare your plan with your partner's and see if you can improve yours or theirs.

Exam question (Paper 2: discussion essay)

Some people say that children from large families are happier. Do you agree?
(120–180 words)

Improving your work

Checking and polishing

Compare your answer with a partner. Go through each other's work. Check for mistakes. Check also the first and last sentences and how the text links together. When your composition is as good as possible, write out a neat copy. Keep your draft and neat copy together in your file.

Learning useful expressions

How do you learn useful words and expressions?

Which of these do you do?

– Write down the English and a translation.
– Write down the English and an explanation in English.
– Write down an example sentence.
– Keep groups of similar new words and phrases together.
– Write new words and phrases on small cards, keep them in a pocket, and look at them frequently.
– Record new words on a cassette which you listen to regularly.
– Write new words on pieces of paper which you stick on the wall in your bedroom.
– Look through your lists of new words regularly so that you don't forget them.
– Try and use the new words when you speak.
– Try and use the new words when you write.

Talk to other people in your class. Find out how they learn new words and expressions.

What new techniques can you use to help your memory?

STUDY TIP 5

Try out as many different learning techniques as you find useful.

Unit 10 A roof over your head

Planning technique: using a questionnaire
Language skills: interpreting abbreviations; expanding and rephrasing information
Exam question: paper 3: directed writing
Improving: self-assessment 2

Preview

What sort of home would you like to live in? Give each of these places listed a number using the scale below according to how much you would like to live there. Then compare your answers with a partner.

cottage	penthouse suite	bamboo hut
bungalow	igloo	log cabin
mansion	palace	castle
cave	caravan	hotel
flat	tent	studio flat

(HATE TO LIVE THERE) 0 ..... 1 ..... 2 ..... 3 ..... 4 ..... 5 ..... 6 ..... 7 ..... 8 ..... 9 ..... 10 (LIKE TO LIVE THERE VERY MUCH)

Planning 1

1 Imagine you and your partner are estate agents. You have to draw up a questionnaire to find out what sort of houses your clients are looking for. Make a list of questions to include on your questionnaire.

Think about:

– type of accommodation
– size
– age
– location
– price
– special features: views, etc.

Examples: What type of accommodation are you looking for? How big should it be?

2 Now find a different partner and interview them about their ideal home.

Interpreting abbreviations

1 Work in pairs. Look at the six house advertisements opposite and decide what the following abbreviations mean:

a) det	c) receps	e) baths	g) ONO	i) £285K	k) Tel:
b) beds	d) GCH	f) Vic	h) C 14th	j) semi-det	

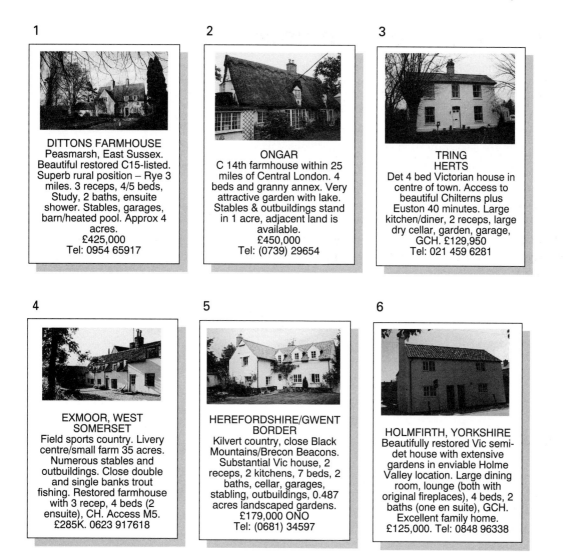

1

DITTONS FARMHOUSE
Peasmarsh, East Sussex.
Beautiful restored C15-listed.
Superb rural position – Rye 3
miles. 3 receps, 4/5 beds,
Study, 2 baths, ensuite
shower. Stables, garages,
barn/heated pool. Approx 4
acres.
£425,000
Tel: 0954 65917

2

ONGAR
C 14th farmhouse within 25
miles of Central London. 4
beds and granny annex. Very
attractive garden with lake.
Stables & outbuildings stand
in 1 acre, adjacent land is
available.
£450,000
Tel: (0739) 29654

3

**TRING
HERTS**
Det 4 bed Victorian house in
centre of town. Access to
beautiful Chilterns plus
Euston 40 minutes. Large
kitchen/diner, 2 receps, large
dry cellar, garden, garage,
GCH. £129,950
Tel: 021 459 6281

4

**EXMOOR, WEST
SOMERSET**
Field sports country. Livery
centre/small farm 35 acres.
Numerous stables and
outbuildings. Close double
and single banks trout
fishing. Restored farmhouse
with 3 recep, 4 beds (2
ensuite), CH. Access M5.
£285K. 0623 917618

5

**HEREFORDSHIRE/GWENT
BORDER**
Kilvert country, close Black
Mountains/Brecon Beacons.
Substantial Vic house, 2
receps, 2 kitchens, 7 beds, 2
baths, cellar, garages,
stabling, outbuildings, 0.487
acres landscaped gardens.
£179,000 ONO
Tel: (0681) 34597

6

HOLMFIRTH, YORKSHIRE
Beautifully restored Vic semi-
det house with extensive
gardens in enviable Holme
Valley location. Large dining
room, lounge (both with
original fireplaces), 4 beds, 2
baths (one en suite), GCH.
Excellent family home.
£125,000. Tel: 0848 96338

2 Do you know what the following common abbreviations mean? Work in pairs. Use a
dictionary to find out as many as you can. Your teacher will help you.

a) e.g.   d) p.m.   g) BA   j) km
b) AD   e) RSVP   h) c.v.   k) PS
c) a.m.   f) a.s.a.p. i) esp.   l) NB

*'What a marvellous view they
have from their surveillance camera!'*

Expanding and rephrasing information

1 Look at the advertisement for the house in Ongar. Study the way the information has been expanded in the passage below. Underline the words which have been added.

We have for sale in Ongar a 14th century farmhouse within 25 miles of Central London. It has four bedrooms and a separate granny annex. There is a very attractive garden with a lake. There are also some stables and outbuildings which stand in one acre of land. Adjacent land is also available. The price is £450,000 and for further information you should telephone (0739) 29654.

2 Now expand the information about the house in Holmfirth, Yorkshire in a similar way.

Planning 2

Using your questions from Planning 1, read the letter below and make notes about the type of accommodation that Janet is looking for.

15 Galway Rd,
Dublin
27th June

Dear Gail,

Thanks for your letter, and thanks for having a look round the estate agents for me. It's ridiculous trying to deal with things at this distance.

Anyway let me just make it clear exactly what I'm looking for.

I don't really mind if it's a house or a flat, and I'm not too fussy about a garden either. It's quite nice to sit out in, in the summer, but you don't do much with it in winter, do you? I really want somewhere with two bedrooms. I don't mind whereabouts in London it is but it must be somewhere quiet - not on a main road or anything like that. And it must have central heating. I'd prefer something old - Victorian or Edwardian maybe - but it must be in a good state of repair. As you know, I'm not into DIY at all. Oh, and price! The most important thing. Well, I can afford up to 130, assuming I'm still on good terms with the building society.

It would be really good if you could sort out a couple of likely places and make appointments to have a look at them on Wednesday afternoon, and then when I arrive we can go straight round and have a look.

Thanks ever so much for your help. By the way, if you can find somewhere that is nice and sunny as well, that would be wonderful - don't ask for much, do I?

See you soon,

Janet

Exam question (Paper 3: directed writing)

Now look at the five advertisements below and complete Gail's reply to Janet on the next page.

1

RURAL IDYLL IN N1
Beautiful garden flat,
beechwood flooring, luxury
teak and pine kitchen,
exposed brickwork, working
fireplace, 2 beds, gch, superb
100' garden. Incredibly quiet.
£107,000 incl. freehold of
entire property.
Tel: 071-942 8966

2

SOHO
STUDIO
W1
Unusually sunny + spacious
2nd floor flat on quiet corner.
Double aspect 21'x18' studio
with five large windows, plus
good sized bathroom &
kitchen with all mod cons.
High ceilings
Immaculate throughout
Ideal pied-a-terre
Entryphone
GCH
135 year lease, very low
outgoings.
£117,500
TEL: 071-792 6594

3

RICHMOND HOUSEBOAT
35ft
Secure, cheap mooring with
shared garden. Double bed,
mains electricity, water,
telephone. Solid fuel stove.
Must be seen.
Bargain at £23,000
Tel: 081-981 5704

4

BLACKHEATH VILLAGE
SE3
Superb 2 bed Victorian
cottage beautifully
modernised, immaculate
decorative condition. Quiet
road in heart of village, 1
minute station, 15 minutes
London Bridge. Suit prof
couple.
£136,000 for quick sale
081-934 5492

5

WIMBLEDON VILLAGE
Bright, sunny 2 bed flat with
separate entrance on upper
ground floor. 2 receps;
original Victorian shutters in
beds; kitchen, bathroom.
GCH. Close Wimbledon
Common in quiet cul-de-sac.
£127,500
081-843 2265 (answerphone)

31, Blenheim Rd
Chelsea
1st July

Dear Janet,
I got some details of a few places from the estate agents today and one of them, in ▬▬▬▬, sounds as if if is almost perfect. It's ▬▬▬▬▬▬▬

▬▬▬▬▬▬▬▬▬▬▬

There was another one which sounded pretty good too. This one is in ▬▬▬ and it's ▬▬▬▬▬

▬▬▬▬▬▬▬▬▬

But it wasn't quite perfect because ▬▬▬▬▬

▬▬▬▬▬▬▬▬▬

▬▬▬▬▬▬▬▬▬

Honestly, these estate agents! They really will send you anything. One of the things they sent was crazy. It was ▬▬▬▬▬

▬▬▬▬▬▬▬▬▬

▬▬▬▬▬▬▬▬▬

Anyway, I've fixed appointments for the first two. Wednesday afternoon at 2:00 and 4:30. And if the first one's as wonderful as it sounds I might be moving too!
See you Wednesday. All the best,

Gail

Improving your work

Checking and polishing

Compare your answer with a partner. Check for mistakes. Look particularly at the way you have expanded the information from the advertisements.

Self-assessment 2

1 Look back at the last few compositions you have written. How do you feel about the standard of your writing? Add to the list in the table below and tick the appropriate boxes.

	Good	*Okay*	*Poor*
Organisation of ideas			
Spelling			
Tenses			
Grammar			
Punctuation			
Vocabulary			
Paragraphing			
....			
....			

Now compare your answers with your self-assessment in Unit 3. Which areas of your writing still need extra work? Your teacher will suggest ways you can improve your weakest areas.

EXAM TIP 22

Get rid of those mistakes quickly – before the exam.

2 How do you feel about your performance on the different types of question in First Certificate? Tick the appropriate boxes.

	Units	*Happy*	*Okay*	*Unhappy*
narratives (stories)	1			
speeches	8			
discursive/expository	5, 9			
descriptions	4			
informal letters	3			
formal letters	7			
Paper 3: directed writing	2, 6, 10			

Which questions do you need to work on most?

Unit 11 **Jobhunting**

Planning technique:	listing questions
Language skills:	recognising topic and illustrative sentences; making applications
Exam question:	paper 2: formal letter
Improving:	planning in the exam

Preview

Arrange these jobs in order of appeal.

pilot   most appealing
stockbroker
teacher
office cleaner
chef
lion tamer
surgeon
banker
confidence trickster
police officer   least appealing

Compare your answers with a partner. Give reasons for your answers. Be prepared to report back on your partner's opinions.

Planning 1

Look at the four job advertisements below. Imagine you are going to interview candidates for these jobs. Work in pairs and make a list of the questions you would ask in each case.

THE BAY TREE
RESTAURANT
HAVE VACANCIES FOR
WAITERS & WAITRESSES
EVENINGS/WEEKENDS
APPLY IN PERSON.

QUALIFIED NANNY WANTED
to look after three children
aged 1–7.
Accommodation & full-board.
Use of car.
Salary & hours to be negotiated.
Please send c.v. & two references to:
Mrs T. Morris, Box 802.

Put the questions into groups according to the kind of information they are trying to find out about the candidate. Compare with another pair how you have grouped your questions and discuss the reasons for your groupings.

Paragraphing: recognising topic and illustrative sentences

Paragraphs are (usually) a series of sentences around a particular topic. When the topic changes, you start a new paragraph.

Study the paragraph below. The underlined sentence is the 'topic sentence', the sentence which introduces the topic, or subject, of the paragraph. The four sentences which follow are 'illustrative sentences', which give more information, more details, examples, to expand on the topic.

I really like my new job. The people I work with are friendly and helpful. The job enables me to travel quite a lot – both in this country and occasionally abroad. Although it's not terribly well paid, it's not too stressful and the holidays are good. This means that I have both the free time and the energy to enjoy lots of interesting hobbies!

1 Find and underline the topic sentence in the paragraph below.

The firm gave me a really good party last Friday. I was retiring after 29 years with the company. I shall be sad to leave all my colleagues and friends. Marjorie has got lots of jobs for me to do in the house – so I don't think I shall be bored.

2 Look at the jumbled letter of application on the next page. Put the paragraphs in the correct order by matching each paragraph with a heading from the table below. Then order the sentences correctly within each paragraph and identify which is the topic sentence in each paragraph. Complete the table with your answers. The first paragraph has been done for you.

Paragraph	Heading	Sentences	Topic sentence
B	Reason for writing	e d	e
....	Qualifications	....	....
....	Experience	....	....
....	Languages	....	....
....	Reason for application	....	....

12 Priory Road
Scarborough
North Yorkshire

19th November 1990

The Personnel Officer
Angus Hotel Group
75–81 Sauchiehall St
Glasgow

Dear Sir or Madam,

A
(a) For the last five years I have been deputy manager at the Scarborough Fiesta.
(b) I have considerable experience in hotel management.
(c) In previous posts I have worked in a wide variety of areas including housekeeping, reception, personnel and restaurant.

B
(d) As you will see from my c.v., I have the qualifications, experience and language proficiency you require.
(e) I would like to apply for the post of Hotel Manager at the Glasgow Angus as advertised in this month's issue of 'The Caterer'.

C
(f) I feel this would be useful in a large international hotel which deals with clients from all over the world.
(g) The first, French, I speak fluently having lived in France for three years.
(h) I also speak good Spanish and some Italian.
(i) I speak three foreign languages well.

D
(j) There are a number of reasons for my applying for this post.
(k) Furthermore, I would like to work in a larger hotel with a more varied and international clientele.
(l) And finally I would also like to live and work in Glasgow – the city where I was brought up as a child and where most of my family and friends still live.
(m) First, having worked as a deputy manager for several years, I now feel ready to take on the challenge and responsibility of being a manager.

E
(n) These included ones on health and hygiene, fire prevention, and interviewing skills and techniques.
(o) I have both an external qualification as well as internal certificates from Fiesta Hotels.
(p) In addition to that, I have attended a number of training courses run by Fiesta Hotels.
(q) Initially I obtained a diploma from the Hotel and Catering Institute of Management Association.

I look forward to hearing from you.

Yours faithfully,

J. D. Ferguson

J. D. Ferguson

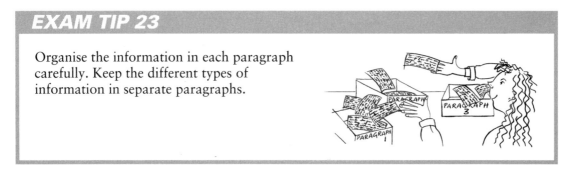

EXAM TIP 23

Organise the information in each paragraph carefully. Keep the different types of information in separate paragraphs.

Making applications

Now look at the complete letter of application on page 72. Underline any words or expressions which you think might be useful in other letters of application.

EXAM TIP 24

Make a note of useful formal expressions that you can use in other letters and be sure to revise them so that you can use them if you have to write a similar letter in the exam.

Planning 2

Look back at the questions you wrote in Planning 1 and answer as many of them as you can about yourself relating to the composition question below. Organise the information into groups as you did in Planning 1.

Exam question (Paper 2: formal letter)

Now write a letter of application for the job advertised below. Remember to set out your letter correctly. Look back at Unit 7 if necessary.

> # TOURIST GUIDES
> **Centrotours (Queensland) Pty** have vacancies in many worldwide locations for full-time local tourist guides.
> Successful applicants will have a good general education, knowledge of their local area, reasonable English, a pleasant manner and the ability to deal with people.
> Please apply in English to:
> The Managing Director, Centrotours, Head Office, PO Box 147, Southport, Queensland 4137.

12 Priory Road
Scarborough
North Yorkshire

19th November 1990

The Personnel Officer
Angus Hotel Group
75–81 Sauchiehall St
Glasgow

Dear Sir/Madam

I would like to apply for the post of Hotel Manager at the Glasgow Angus as advertised in this month's issue of 'The Caterer'. As you will see from my c.v., I have the qualifications, experience and language proficiency you require.

I have both an external qualification and internal certificates from Fiesta Hotels. Initially I obtained a diploma from the Hotel and Catering Institute of Management Association. In addition to that, I have attended a number of training courses run by Fiesta Hotels. These included ones on health and hygiene, fire prevention, and interviewing skills and techniques.

I have considerable experience in hotel management. For the last five years I have been deputy manager at the Scarborough Fiesta. In previous posts I have worked in a wide variety of areas including housekeeping, reception, personnel and restaurant.

I speak three foreign languages well. The first, French, I speak fluently, having lived in France for three years. I also speak good Spanish and some Italian. I feel this would be useful in a large international hotel which deals with clients from all over the world.

There are a number of reasons for my applying for this post. First, having worked as a deputy manager for several years, I now feel ready to take on the challenge and responsibility of being a manager. Furthermore, I would like to work in a larger hotel with a more varied and international clientele. And finally I would also like to live and work in Glasgow – the city where I was brought up as a child and where most of my family and friends still live.

I look forward to hearing from you.

Yours faithfully

J. D. Ferguson

J. D. Ferguson

Now turn back to Exam Tip 24 on page 71.

Improving your work

Checking and polishing

Compare your letter with your partner's. Check for mistakes. Look particularly at the organisation of the paragraphs, the structure of each paragraph, and the language used.

Planning in the exam

1 In the exam you have 45 minutes for each composition. How will you divide that time between planning, writing, and improving?

One possibility is:

    planning – 10 minutes   writing – 30 minutes   improving – 5 minutes

Whatever you do, the planning phase is going to be much shorter than usual. It is therefore a good idea to get used to planning compositions quickly. It is also a good idea if you use your planning time to write down some of the words and expressions that you are going to use in your composition.

You might divide your time like this:

    thinking of ideas – 4 minutes
    organising ideas into paragraphs – 3 minutes
    noting useful words and expressions – 3 minutes

On your own decide:

– how you will divide up your time for each composition.
– how you will divide up your planning time.

2 Now plan compositions for one or two of these titles in the time you have allowed yourself:

1 Your teacher is leaving to become the Head of a new school in a neighbouring town. You have been asked to make a speech thanking them for their hard work and wishing them luck in their new job. Write what you would say.

2 You have been on holiday in your country for a couple of weeks. Write a letter to a penfriend telling them what you have been doing.

3 'Keeping pets inside one's house is a disgusting practice.' Discuss.

4 Write a story that ends with the words ' . . . the little boy ran up the stairs shouting, "He's here! He's here!" '

EXAM TIP 25

Use your time wisely in the exam. Get used to planning quickly and thoroughly. Decide now how much time you'll spend on writing and planning in the exam.

Unit 12 Getaway

Planning technique:	using a 'spidergraph'
Language skills:	organising descriptions; prepositions following adjectives
Exam question:	paper 2: description
Improving:	checking and polishing in the exam

Preview

Work in groups of six. Choose one of the following holidays for each member of the group. Persuade the other members of the group to let you have the holiday you want.

- a cruise down the River Nile
- a month on a Pacific island
- a Kenyan safari
- a camel journey across the Sahara
- a week in the European capital of their choice
- a cycling holiday in the Himalayas

Planning 1

A 'spidergraph' (see Unit 4) is often a useful way of noting down information about places. Complete this diagram using the words in the box opposite, and adding some ideas of your own.

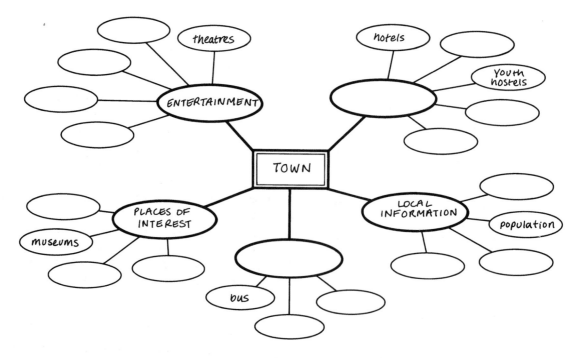

nightclubs	train	history	bed and breakfast	art galleries	travel
cinemas	accommodation	architecture	guest houses	monuments	discos

Organising descriptions

1 Read the text and answer the questions that follow.

No matter from what direction you approach the Potala, it always appears unspoilt by its surroundings – it looks as if it had nothing to do with them, floating there on its mountainside. To its west the Chinese quarter is little more than an industrial estate. To the east a small valley hides much of the city, to give the villages on that side a view of their palace. Inside Lhasa itself, you could rarely lose sight of it.

The present palace was built in the mid seventeenth century by the great Fifth Dalai Lama, and it took thousands of workers half a century to complete. Standing over a hundred metres up, it is reached by a series of switchbacks, the steps hidden from view. Its entrance is an enormous double door concealed by a vast curtain. Wide stairs lead up from it through a passageway, and here you notice that the outer walls of the palace are several feet thick. The passageway takes you to an open courtyard overlooked by the Dalai Lama's living quarters.

It is a maze of rooms, altars, temples, halls and passageways. From everywhere there are magnificent views over Lhasa. The workmanship here is superb down to the smallest detail. Influences are many: here one could detect that of Iran, there that of China. Red and gold are the dominant colours.

The rooms are decorated with rich materials, tapestries and paintings, the detail of whose work one cannot describe, the pictures telling stories of heroes and the gods, or simply showing views of the local landscape, with Lhasa and the Potala in prominent positions. The candles below them light up the faces of the golden statues of Buddha in all his forms.

And at the very heart of the palace is its heart indeed – the enormous chamber containing the tombs of the former Dalai Lamas. The biggest shrines are those of the Fifth and the Thirteenth Dalai Lamas – the former is covered with 300,000 ounces of gold.

(adapted from *Danziger's Travels:* Nick Danziger. Paladin. 1988)

1 What does the writer describe in a) the first paragraph?
                                           b) the second paragraph?
                                           c) the third paragraph?
                                           d) the fourth paragraph?
                                           e) the last paragraph?
2 Why do you think he has followed this order?
3 Do you think he began with the most important thing?
4 Which adjectives has he used to describe the palace?
5 Which senses has he focused most on: sight, sound, taste, smell, etc.?
6 What do you think is the best part of the description?

2 Think of a famous place near where you are now. Discuss with a partner and make notes about how you would organise a description of it.

EXAM TIP 26

The text gives one example of how to organise descriptions. You and your classmates have probably thought of other ways.
Remember – organise your writing.

Prepositions following adjectives

1 Look at the text on page 75 and find prepositions to complete the phrases below.

unspoilt .... its surroundings

hidden .... view

concealed .... a vast curtain

decorated .... rich materials

covered .... 300,000 ounces of gold

*'Isn't it exciting, Ralph, I've never been
this far from a McDonald's before ...'*

2 Now look at the following sentences. Fill the blank in each with one of the following prepositions.

> to   of   for   with

1 She was very pleased .... her holiday photos.
2 Local people are often very generous .... foreigners who pass through their village.
3 Boats between the islands are quite capable .... arriving a day late or even more.
4 The scenery here is similar .... that in the south of the country.
5 The tour company were responsible .... our luggage.
6 I became extremely angry .... them when our suitcase disappeared.
7 The architectural style of this palace is related .... that of the early fifth century Greek temples.
8 I suddenly became aware .... someone trying to take my wallet out of my pocket.
9 Going on a cruise is not suitable .... people who get bored easily.

3 Tell your partner about:

– a place you are familiar ....
– a type of transport you are fond ....
– something your family is famous ....

Now complete the boxes below:

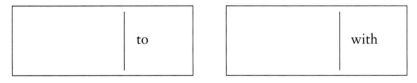

| | to |
| | |

| | with |
| | |

| | of |
| | |

| | for |
| | |

Add other adjectives to the boxes as you come across them in the next few weeks.

Remember that some adjectives can take different prepositions in other contexts.

Planning 2

Look at the exam question below and draw a 'spidergraph' including on it all the information relevant to your answer.

Compare your plan with a partner.

Exam question (Paper 2: description)

Describe the place where you spent the most enjoyable holiday of your life, saying why you enjoyed it.

Improving your work

Checking and polishing

Compare your letter with a partner. Check for mistakes. Look particularly at the way the description is organised and the use of prepositions.

Checking and polishing in the exam

You will not have time in the exam to write out a neat copy, so now is the time to start writing your compositions only once. You will have to do the checking and polishing and make any changes to your first copy.

Make sure that you make any alterations neatly and legibly. Make quite sure that it is clear to the examiners which is the correct version, and which is crossed out.

If necessary, write on alternate lines so that you have enough room for corrections.

Go through your work systematically. Look for the mistakes that you know you make the most often.

How long will *you* need for checking and polishing? Decide now. Make sure you leave enough time.

Unit 13 Crime doesn't pay

Planning technique:	opening sentences
Language skills:	using direct speech in narratives; making your writing more interesting
Exam question:	paper 2: narrative
Improving:	writing the correct number of words in the exam

Preview

Work in groups of three or four. Look at the sentences below. Decide if you agree or disagree. If you disagree, change the sentence so that every member of the group agrees with it.

a) All murderers should be executed.

b) Corporal punishment should be reintroduced for certain crimes.

c) People who drink and drive should lose their driving licences for ever.

d) It should be illegal for parents to smack their children.

e) Prisons should be as uncomfortable as possible.

f) Judges should retire at the age of 60.

Planning 1

Read the passages below. Each contains the first sentences of a novel. Work in pairs and discuss how you think the plots in the various books develop.

A   The woman was lying dead on the floor when he came in. She was already dead and covered up from head to toe but Wexford only knew that afterwards, not at the time. He looked back and realised the chances he had missed but it was useless doing that – he hadn't known and that was all.

B   I met the boy on the morning of the kidnapping. It was a bright and blowing day. The wind was fresh from the sea, and the piled white cubes of the city sparkled under a swept blue sky. I had to force myself to go to work.

C   Tom glanced behind him and saw the man coming out of the Green Cage, heading his way. Tom walked faster. There was no doubt that the man was after him. Tom had noticed him five minutes ago, eyeing him carefully from a table, as if he weren't quite sure, but almost. He had looked sure enough for Tom to down his drink in a hurry, pay and get out.

Using direct speech in narratives

1 Work in pairs. Look at the passage below and then choose the best answers to the questions which follow.

When Saltfleet came back from shopping, three hours later, Geraldine was sitting on the doorstep. He was delighted, but then immediately began to worry.

'What are you doing here?'

She kissed him. 'I got bored so I thought I'd come and see you and Mummy,' she explained.

They went into the kitchen, and he unloaded his purchases on the table. Geraldine opened the refrigerator and poured herself a glass of milk.

'I'm dying of hunger . . . Are you doing anything nice this afternoon?'

'We thought we'd go to Regent's Park and have tea there.'

'Oh good! Can we go to the zoo?'

'I expect so.'

1 What are inverted commas (' ') used for?

   a) to stress words
   b) to show which words are actually spoken
   c) to show who is speaking

2 Which of the following can separate the spoken words from other words?

   a) a comma
   b) a question mark
   c) a full stop
   d) an exclamation mark
   e) nothing

3 Where is the punctuation mark separating the spoken words from the words which follow?

   a) inside the inverted commas
   b) outside the inverted commas

4 When is a new line started?

   a) whenever someone speaks
   b) when the speaker changes
   c) for each new sentence

5 When is a paragraph indented?

   a) only when it starts with narrative
   b) only when it starts with direct speech
   c) both

2 Work in pairs and use what you have just found out about direct speech in narrative to punctuate the passage below.

> You don't like me much do you Inspector. I wouldn't say that replied Morse defensively. It's just that you've never got into the habit of telling me the truth have you. I've made up for it now I hope. Have you. Morse's eyes were hard and piercing, but to his question there was no reply. Shall I sign it now. Morse remained silent for a while. You think it's better this way he asked very quietly. But again there was no reply, and Morse passed across the statement and stood up. You've got a pen. Sheila Phillipson nodded, and opened her long, expensive leather handbag.

EXAM TIP 27

Make sure you know the rules for punctuating direct speech. Using direct speech can make a narrative vivid and more interesting.

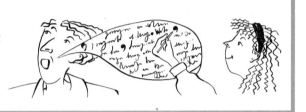

Making your writing more interesting

1 Look at passage C in Planning 1. How many different words can you find to do with the verb *see*?

2 You will make your writing considerably more interesting if you do not always use the simple words such as *walk*, *say* and *see*. There are plenty more descriptive words in English that you can use.

Look at the word squares below, find as many words as you can that mean something similar to the word that has been circled and write them below. You will find the words horizontally, diagonally and vertically.

```
W A L K S H X       P R O M I S E       G L I M P S E
A R P R T U T       S Z L A N U A       L A O Z Q T N
N U S U R R I       A H Y R S G D       A E Z O L A O
D N Q S O R P       Y P O G I G V       N N Y E K R T
E A L H L Y T       A C C U S E I       C P Q E M E I
R M S X L V O       V S Q E T S S       E W A T C H C
Z O C H A S E       O A D M I T E       P E E R X S E
```

walk	*say*	*look*

3 Now work in pairs and rewrite the passage below to make it sound more interesting.

   Hopkins walked into the bar and sat down. He looked round but no one was looking at him. The barman walked up.
   'Beer,' said Hopkins.
   'Budweiser?' said the barman.
   'Yes,' said Hopkins.
   Just then a man walked into the bar. Hopkins turned and looked at him. The man walked up to the bar. 'You can keep the beer,' he said to the barman. Turning to Hopkins, he said, 'I'm Goodman. West Sussex Police. You're under arrest.'

EXAM TIP 28

Using a variety of language will show your range of vocabulary and structure and make your writing more interesting.

Planning 2

Look at the question below. Think of a good first sentence or two and write them down. Exchange sentences with a partner and speculate as to how the plot might develop. When you have exchanged ideas, draw a flow diagram (see Unit 1) to illustrate how you will develop the story.

Exam question (Paper 2: narrative)

Write a story that ends with the words:

   . . . she felt a hand on her shoulder and heard a voice say, 'Lisa Altman. I arrest you in the name of the law.'

(120–180 words)

"OK, sergeant, Scotland Yard'll handle it now—
where exactly was the body found?"

Improving your work

Checking and polishing

Remember your time limit for checking in the exam. Check through your work within the time limit. Look particularly at your use of language and your punctuation of direct speech.

Length in the exam

'The question paper asks for 120–180 words. How many words should I write?'

Less than 120 words: Too short. You will lose marks if you write less than you should. For example, if you write 90 words (three-quarters of the length), your best possible mark will be 15 out of 20 (three-quarters of the total marks).

120–150 words: Okay. A lot will depend on the quality of what you write. However, you probably haven't written enough to be able to show the examiners quite how good your writing is.

150–180 words: Very good. Just the right length and you have given yourself enough space to show how well you can write.

180–200 words: Good. The extra few words won't count against you and they may help the general impression that your answer will create. The examiners will only mark the first 180 words. However, they can give credit for anything extra that is relevant. So if you need them to finish what you are writing, that is okay.

Over 200 words: Too long. The extra words won't count against you, and they may possibly add to the general impression of your answer. However, you will have wasted a lot of time writing more words than you needed to when you could have spent that time checking the 180 words that are important.

Note: The examiner will not count the words in your composition but he or she will immediately realise if your composition is too short or too long. You will probably know without counting the words how much you need to write. However, if you want to feel safe, count them.

EXAM TIP 29

Write the correct number of words, but don't waste too much time counting. Have an idea of what 150–180 words looks like in your handwriting.

Unit 14 Good sports

Planning technique:	deciding priorities
Language skills:	combining information; verbs which take gerund and/or infinitive
Exam question:	paper 3: directed writing
Improving:	reading and answering the question

Preview

Work in pairs or small groups. Decide if the following are sports or games or neither.

chess   football   fishing   rowing   table tennis
crosswords   swimming   hunting   juggling   jogging
karate   cycling   yoga   bridge   poker

Try and define a sport and a game.

Planning 1

What, for you, are the most important aspects of any sport or leisure activity? Number the sentences below in order of priority (1 = most important .... 10 = least important). When you have finished compare your answer with a partner.

- ☐ It must be cheap.
- ☐ It must make me think.
- ☐ It must involve hard physical activity.
- ☐ It must involve meeting other people socially.
- ☐ It must be something I can do on my own or with only a few other people.
- ☐ I must be able to do it at or near my home.
- ☐ It must be competitive.
- ☐ It must be a ball game.
- ☐ It must be something I can continue to do when I get older.
- ☐ It must involve animals.

Combining information

Read the two leaflets and summarise the information in the table on page 86.

BARTON SPORTS CENTRE – SUMMER PROGRAMME

There are some places left on our Summer Sports programme. If you would like further information, call Mandy on (0342) 787000 or call in at the Centre – 99, Richfield Avenue.

There are a few places left in the two CYCLING squads – Wednesday afternoons 3–5; or Friday evenings 6–8.

The FOOTBALL team meets on Tuesday evenings for training and Friday evenings for a match and they are always looking for new talent.

SQUASH courts are available every evening from 6 o'clock onwards and there are always people around looking for a game. Tutors are available too during this time.

The joggers go JOGGING every afternoon from 3 o'clock and new members are always welcome to join them.

Come along and join us.

Too fat? Get fit at
The Ken Newton
Health and Fitness Centre

There are a few places left on some of our new season's courses. ENROL NOW.

- YOGA: the relaxing way to improve your physical and mental fitness. Come along on a Monday morning (10 a.m.) or a Tuesday evening (6 p.m.)
- JUDO: the classic art of self-defence will tone up your body, sharpen your mind and increase your self-confidence. Tuesday morning at 11, or Monday evening at 7 p.m.
- AEROBICS: music, movement and muscle tone. Fun and fitness at the same time. Come and join us on a Thursday. Mornings at 11, evenings at 8.
- BADMINTON: If you don't know how to play, come along and learn. Wednesday evenings only – from 6 p.m.
- WEIGHTS: For real strength and muscle building, use our facilities any weekday afternoon between 2 and 5. Expert guidance on hand to help you decide on a suitable programme.

THE KEN NEWTON FITNESS CENTRE
WHERE FITNESS MATTERS

3, Coley Avenue, West Barton. Tel: (0342) 453980

	Monday	*Tuesday*	*Wednesday*	*Thursday*	*Friday*
morning				*aerobics 11am*	
afternoon					
evening			*badminton from 6pm*		

Verbs which take the gerund and/or infinitive

1 Look at the following pairs of sentences. Underline the –ing and infinitive forms.

Find the incorrect sentences. (Sometimes both sentences in a pair are right.) Look at the other sentences and decide if there is any difference in meaning when the verb is followed by a gerund and when it's followed by an infinitive.

1 a) He began to run after the doctor had told him to get fit.
  b) She began running in 1975 when she went to school.

2 a) She isn't very keen on sport generally, but she enjoys swimming.
  b) She enjoys to swim in the morning when the pool is empty.

3 a) They tried to walk faster but the wind was too strong.
  b) Their feet were cold so they tried walking faster.

4 a) When I got to the top of the hill I stopped to look at the view.
  b) When I noticed the time, I stopped looking at the view and set off home.

5 a) Jim promised to play football with me on Saturday afternoon.
  b) Although the weather was terrible, he promised playing football with me.

6 a) She continued cycling even though her legs ached.
  b) She continued to cycle until she was 86.

2 Now put the verbs from the sentences above into one of the boxes below.

verbs which only take –ing	verbs which only take **to + infinitive**
verbs which take **–ing** or **to + infinitive** with no change in meaning	verbs which take **–ing** or **to + infinitive** with a change in meaning

3 Now write down:

- a sport you enjoy doing
- something you never remember to do
- a place you want to visit
- a book you intend to read
- a terrible meal you remember eating

Compare your answers with a partner.

Now add these verbs to the boxes above. Continue adding (to add) verbs as you come across them.

Planning 2

Read the information in the exam question below. Decide which activity each person should take up. When you have decided, compare your answer with a partner.

Exam question (Paper 3: directed writing)

Study the information below. Then complete the paragraphs opposite. Write about 50 words for each paragraph.

Activity	Cost	Exercise
Yoga	*	*
Judo	**	**
Weight training	**	***
Aerobics	*	**
Badminton	**	***
Jogging	*	**
Cycling	***	***
Football	**	***
Squash	**	***

	Monday	Tuesday	Wednesday	Thursday	Friday
morning	yoga 10 am	Judo 11am		aerobics 11am	
afternoon	weight training 2-5 Jogging from 3pm	weight Training 2-5 Jogging from 3pm	weight Training 2-5 Jogging from 3pm cycling 3-5	weight Training 2-5 Jogging from 3pm	weight Training 2-5 Jogging from 3pm
evening	squash from 6 Judo 7pm	squash from 6 yoga 6pm football Training	squash from 6 badminton from 6pm	squash from 6 aerobics 8pm	squash from 6 cycling 6-8 football match

Ann Wilkins looks after her three children at home. She would like to do some sort of activity to improve her fitness but she can only do it one afternoon a week when she can get a friend to look after the children for her. She doesn't mind how expensive it is.

Brian Phillips is unemployed. He would like to take up a sport in the afternoons to keep himself busy. As he is unemployed, he would like it to be something very cheap.

Carol Davis is a dentist. She usually works in the afternoons and evenings so she would like to do something in the mornings. She hasn't done any sort of sport for about ten years so she would like to do something fairly easy to start with.

Daniel Carter is a writer. He spends most of the day working at home and would like to take up some sort of team game that gets him out of the house in the evenings. He doesn't want to go out more than two or three evenings a week.

I think Ann Wilkins should take up .... because

....

....

....

....

It would be best for Brian Phillips to take up ....because

....

....

....

In my opinion Carol Davis should try .... because

....

....

....

....

I believe that Daniel Carter would like .... because

....

....

....

....

Improving your work

Checking and polishing

Remember your time limit for checking in the exam. Decide how long you will allow for checking the directed writing question. Check through your work within that time limit. Look particularly at the use of gerunds and infinitives.

Reading and answering the question

Look at the question and the students' answers below. Which students read the question properly? Which students answered the question fully? Which students do you think will get the highest marks? Discuss your answers.

> Write a paragraph about a memorable sports event you have been to. Say what it was, where you went, why it was memorable, and what your feelings were at the time.

1   I went with my parents to the Olympic Games in Seoul in 1988. We enjoyed it very much, especially the athletics. I like the pole vault best – it's amazing that they can jump so high! We stayed in a nice hotel and ate lots of Korean food.

2   Last year my brother ran in the New York marathon. I went to see him run and it was very exciting. There were thousands of runners, and lots of handicapped people racing in wheelchairs too. My brother didn't win, but he was pleased that he finished it.

3   The best sports event I ever went to was a tennis match at Wimbledon in 1980, between Björn Borg and John McEnroe. It was really exciting. One set ended in a tie break that went on for a very long time. The whole crowd was excited. I am Swedish so I felt very pleased that finally Björn Borg won.

EXAM TIP 30

Remember to read the question carefully and answer everything the question asks you. Underline the important parts of the question so that you don't forget to answer them.

Unit 15 Customer relations

Planning technique:	selecting relevant information
Language skills:	linking words for attitude; the past in sequence
Exam question:	paper 2: formal letter
Improving:	brief and accurate writing

Preview

Tick your answers on the questionnaire below and then work out your score. Compare your answers with a partner.

HOW GOOD ARE YOU AT COMPLAINING?

1 **You order soup in a restaurant.**
   When it arrives it is cold. What do you do?
   A Eat it and say nothing.
   B Call the waiter and send it back.
   C Say nothing but don't leave a tip.

2 **You have some photos developed. When you**
   take them out of the envelope, you notice that
   the colour reproduction is poor. What do you do?
   A Blame yourself for being a bad photographer.
   B Take them back to the shop and ask them to try again.
   C Say nothing but take your next film somewhere else.

3 **You buy a bottle of milk at your local supermarket. When you try it,**
   it tastes horrible. What do you do?
   A Throw it away.
   B Take it back and ask for another bottle.
   C Drink it anyway.

4 **You buy a sweater at a big department store. When you get home,**
   you notice it has a small hole under the arm. What do you do?
   A Nothing. Nobody will notice it.
   B Take it back and ask to change it.
   C Mend the hole.

Score 3 points for each B, 1 point for each C, 0 points for each A.

10 and over: What a grouch! You complain about absolutely everything. Try to get a sense of proportion.

6-9: You have a reasonable attitude to life and know when something is important enough to complain about.

0-5: Come on! Be more assertive! At the moment you let people walk all over you.

Planning 1

You have had a terrible meal in a restaurant and are about to write to the manager to complain. Look at the list of points below and cross out those which you would not mention in your letter.

- The soup was cold.
- My wife was wearing her new dress.
- The table wasn't ready when we arrived.
- Lobster was not on the menu.
- The 'fresh' prawns were frozen.
- The napkins did not match the tablecloth.
- Our table was near the door to the street.
- The person at the next table was smoking.
- The service was slow.
- We had to wait 35 minutes for our first course.
- The waiter was rude to me.
- The waiter was not wearing a tie.
- The wine waiter spilt wine on my trousers.
- We had to wait 30 minutes to get the bill.

'Tonight's specials are: Sweetbreads en Brochette, Lobster à l' Americaine and Brook Trout Meunière. And tonight's topic of conversation is: the slow service.'

Linking words for attitude

Read this letter of complaint and cross out the two wrong options in each box.

43 Wimbledon Ave
Wendover
Bucks HW3 5TQ

23rd March 1991

The Manager
Plum Tree Restaurant
Hampstead Court
Wendover
Bucks

Dear Sir,

I am writing to complain about the meal we had at your restaurant last Saturday.

It was, | personally, 1 / to be honest, / naturally, | not what I expect from a restaurant with your reputation. We arrived at

7.30, having booked a table earlier by phone. | To my surprise 2 / Fortunately / To make matters worse | the head waiter had no knowledge of our booking.

Clearly, 3
Fortunately,
Obviously,

or perhaps

unfortunately,
apparently,
naturally, 4

the restaurant was not full and we were able to stay.

When we had ordered our meal, the waiter told us there would be a short delay. It was then 7.45. We sat and waited for our first course until 8.45.

Clearly 5
Fortunately
Personally

I feel that an hour is too long to wait for one's first course.

Apparently 6
To be honest
Naturally

you do not.

Moving on to the food, the menu had stated that the soup was 'homemade' but it

fortunately 7
clearly
to make matters worse

came from a tin. We also ordered 'fresh' prawns but these were

personally
naturally
obviously 8

not fresh, as they were still frozen in the middle.

To make matters worse,
To be honest,
Clearly, 9

when we tried to complain the staff seemed to take no interest at all.

Naturally 10
Apparently
Fortunately

I do not feel that the service or the food was worth the £48.90 that we had to pay. I am therefore enclosing a copy of the bill and I would be grateful if you would send me a complete refund as soon as possible.

Yours faithfully,

Aileen Snaith

Aileen Snaith (Mrs)

EXAM TIP 31

Use linking words to make your writing more fluent.

The past in sequence

1 Study these two sentences from the letter on page 93.

1 When we had ordered our meal, the waiter told us there would be a short delay.
2 When we tried to complain, the staff seemed to take no interest at all.

Why is *when* followed by the past perfect in sentence 1, but by the simple past in sentence 2? In which sentence can you put *after* instead of *when*? Discuss your answer with a partner.

2 Now join these sentences together with *when* or *after*. You may need to change the tense.

1 She saw the fly in her soup. She complained.
2 The waiter brought my steak. The head waiter asked if everything was all right.
3 She saw the advertisement in the estate agent's window. She went in and asked about the flat.
4 The plane took off. The terrorists announced there was a bomb on board.
5 We took our washing to the launderette. We had a cup of coffee.
6 Our washing finished. We took it out of the machine.
7 I saw the dog in front of me on the pavement. I crossed over the road.
8 I picked up the newspaper. I saw the result of the election.
9 She arrived at the hotel. She registered at reception.

Planning 2

Look at the exam question. Write down five important points that you should include in your letter and five points that you do not think you should include. Look back at Planning 1 for some ideas if you need to. Make sure you mix up the points.

Now exchange lists with a partner and see if they can identify which are the five points to be included.

Exam question (Paper 2: formal letter)

You sent for the jacket shown in the advertisement opposite, but when it arrived it was not what you expected. Write a letter of complaint to the manufacturer, saying what is wrong with the jacket and what you want them to do about it. Your letter should be polite but firm.

Stay dry while you work or play!!
WATERPROOF, BREATHABLE JACKET

The WEATHERMAN jacket is made from a revolutionary new fabric and is guaranteed 100% waterproof. The special fleecy cotton lining keeps you warm while the fantastic outer jacket keeps you dry – whatever the weather!

* Fleecy cotton lining to keep you warm
* Taped seams make it totally waterproof
* Strong, heavy-duty zip fastener
* Two large pockets with stud fasteners
* Large zipped map pocket at front
* Detachable hood
* Tightly-fitting cuffs to keep hands warm and dry
* Can be washed or dry-cleaned
* Sizes to fit everyone – 36" 40" 44" 48"
* Attractive dark blue or dark green

At the amazing price of £42.50 (includes postage)

Weatherman Clothing Company, 1B Ash Rd, Green Lanes Estate,

Not 100% waterproof - lets in heavy rain
Zip is not strong - broke after only 3 days
Zipped map pocket is too small for a map
Hood is not detachable
Horrible bright green colour

Improving your work

Checking and polishing

Remember your time limit for checking in the exam. Check through your work within the time limit. Look particularly at the sequence of tenses, and at any words you have used to convey attitude.

Brief and accurate writing

Look at these three passages from letters of complaint. Which do you think is best and why?

1 I bought a Radioki 345K from your shop which had its volume control knob missing.

2 Last Wednesday I bought a Radioki cassette player (Model no: 345K) from your shop. When I got home, I discovered that the volume control knob was missing.

3 Last Wednesday, 14ᵗʰ August 1991, I came into your shop and, after looking at a number of different models, I bought a blue Radioki cassette player (Model no: 345K). I finished my other shopping and when I got home later in the afternoon, I discovered that one of the knobs on the top - the one which controls how loud it is - was missing.

EXAM TIP 32

Keep your writing as brief and accurate as possible. Don't leave out important information. Don't put in unnecessary information.

Unit 16 Eat it!

Planning technique:	'brainstorming'
Language skills:	giving instructions; linking words for instructions
Exam question:	paper 2: speech
Improving:	managing time in the exam

Preview

Match the words to each picture.

chop   slice   peel   boil   fry   sprinkle   stir   whisk
spread   apple   bread   orange   egg   fish   breadcrumbs
coffee   cream   butter

Planning 1

'Brainstorming'

You have:
– three minutes to think of and list the names of as many fruits and vegetables as you can.
– two minutes to think of and list the names of as many different kinds of meat as you can.
– two minutes to think of and list as many other different kinds of food as you can.

Giving instructions

1 Read the text and fill each blank with the correct form of one of the verbs from the lists below.

Raspberry, Apple and Mint Sauce

450 g raspberries
450 g apples (weighed after peeling, coring and chopping small)
900 g sugar
200 ml finely chopped fresh mint

First ▮▮▮▮▮ (1) the raspberries in a large saucepan and ▮▮▮▮▮ (2) them gently over a low heat until the juice ▮▮▮▮▮ (3) to run. Then ▮▮▮▮▮ (4) the apples and ▮▮▮▮▮ (5) to cook very gently until the apple ▮▮▮▮▮ (6) to a pulp.

Right, well after that you ▮▮▮▮▮ (7) the sugar in and you ▮▮▮▮▮ (8) it over a gentle heat. Now when all the sugar ▮▮▮▮▮ (9), you ▮▮▮▮▮ (10) the mint. Next you ▮▮▮▮▮ (11) everything up quickly and you ▮▮▮▮▮ (12) on boiling it for about 5 or 10 minutes. Then you ▮▮▮▮▮ (13) the sauce cool for about half an hour. After that you ▮▮▮▮▮ (14) it a stir to mix the mint in evenly and then you ▮▮▮▮▮ (15) it into clean warm jars. Finally, when it's cool, you ▮▮▮▮▮ (16) the jars and ▮▮▮▮▮ (17) them. Mmm! It's really delicious – especially with chicken and things like that!

1	a) add	b) place	c) let
2	a) warm	b) begin	c) keep
3	a) begin	b) let	c) put
4	a) put	b) stir	c) add
5	a) boil	b) continue	c) let
6	a) cook	b) put	c) pour
7	a) put	b) place	c) keep
8	a) add	b) continue	c) stir
9	a) warm	b) boil	c) dissolve
10	a) put	b) add	c) place
11	a) boil	b) warm	c) pour
12	a) let	b) keep	c) add
13	a) begin	b) put	c) let
14	a) give	b) begin	c) add
15	a) label	b) add	c) pour
16	a) dissolve	b) seal	c) place
17	a) label	b) put	c) cook

2 Look at the two paragraphs in the recipe. Which is more likely to be spoken English? Which is more likely to be written? Why?

EXAM TIP 33

Remember which verb forms to use in spoken and written instructions. In written English the verbs are more likely to be in the **imperative,** 'Place the raspberries in a large saucepan'; in spoken English, the instructions are more likely to be given with **you + present tense,** ' . . . after that you put the sugar in . . . '

"Open up! It's the Police!"

Linking words for instructions

1 Read the text on page 98 again and list all the linking words used.

2 Now rewrite the recipe below as a continuous spoken text, putting in linking words where appropriate.

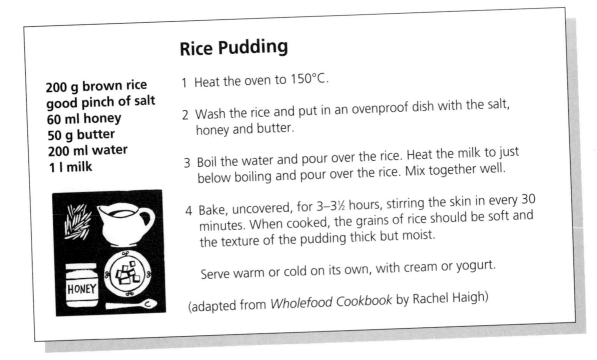

Rice Pudding

200 g brown rice
good pinch of salt
60 ml honey
50 g butter
200 ml water
1 l milk

1 Heat the oven to 150°C.

2 Wash the rice and put in an ovenproof dish with the salt, honey and butter.

3 Boil the water and pour over the rice. Heat the milk to just below boiling and pour over the rice. Mix together well.

4 Bake, uncovered, for 3–3½ hours, stirring the skin in every 30 minutes. When cooked, the grains of rice should be soft and the texture of the pudding thick but moist.

Serve warm or cold on its own, with cream or yogurt.

(adapted from *Wholefood Cookbook* by Rachel Haigh)

Planning 2

Look at the composition question below and write down 25 words and ideas that you will need for your composition.

Now use another planning technique to order what you have written.

Exam question (Paper 2: speech)

You meet a group of English people on holiday who ask you how to cook a traditional dish from your country. Write what you would say.

Improving your work

Checking and polishing

Remember your time limit for checking in the exam. Check through your work within the time limit. Look particularly at the verb tenses and the linking words.

Managing time in the exam

You should now have done some timed practice questions and be aware of how long it takes you to plan, write and check your exam answers. Now is the time to make any final changes to your plan.

In Paper 2 you have to write two compositions of 120–180 words in 1½ hours.

Fill in your time plan below.

Activity	Minutes
reading the paper and choosing which two questions to answer	....
first composition: planning	....
writing	....
checking	....
second composition: planning	....
writing	....
checking	....
final check	....

In Paper 3 you have six questions including the directed writing question. You have two hours for the whole paper.

– What order will you do the questions in?
– How long will you allow for each question?

Fill in your time plan below.

Activity	Minutes
planning your answer to the directed writing question	....
writing your answer	....
checking your answer	....

EXAM TIP 34

Make sure your time plan is clear before you go into the exam. It can be flexible; but it must exist.

Unit 17 **Stay healthy!**

Planning technique:	using boxes for categories
Language skills:	writing a paragraph; inversion
Exam question:	paper 2: discussion essay
Improving:	checking in the exam

Preview

Find someone in your class who:

- has never been to hospital   ....
- is a vegetarian   ....
- takes some sort of exercise every day ....
- hasn't had a cold for two years   ....
- always goes to bed before midnight ....

Planning 1

1 Look at this composition question.

> What do you think are the main reasons that people live longer now than 100 years ago?

Add to the notes below:

Medical care	Diet
– improved facilities – available to more people – people are more aware –	– people eat more healthily – – –
Fitness	*Education*
– – – –	– – – –

2 When you have finished your notes, compare them with a partner and discuss how you would organise your composition.

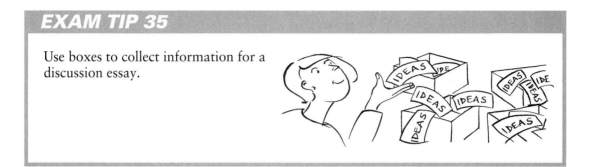

EXAM TIP 35

Use boxes to collect information for a discussion essay.

Writing a paragraph

1 Look at the paragraph below and match the correct label to each sentence.

> One of the main reasons that people live longer is that there has been considerable progress in the field of medical care. Not only have knowledge and facilities improved but medical services are also available to more people than ever before. Many countries, for example, have national health systems which provide free treatment for the whole population. In addition to this, people have become more aware of the importance of staying healthy. As a result, they take greater care of themselves and thus avoid many fatal illnesses and diseases.

Sentence 1	example of illustration 2
Sentence 2	illustration 3
Sentence 3	result of illustration 3
Sentence 4	illustrations 1 and 2
Sentence 5	topic sentence

Paragraphs usually consist of a topic sentence (see Unit 11) and illustrations and development of the point made in the topic sentence.

2 Looking at your notes in Planning 1, write another paragraph that might appear in your answer to the composition question.

When you have written it, exchange paragraphs with your partner and see if they can label each sentence in a similar way to the exercise above.

EXAM TIP 36

Think about how you organise your sentences into paragraphs.

Inversion

1 Study this sentence taken from the paragraph in exercise 1 on page 103.

> Not only have knowledge and facilities improved but medical services are also available to more people than ever before.

The writer could also have put:

> Knowledge and facilities have not only improved but medical services are also available to more people than ever before.

What is the difference between these two sentences?

2 In each sentence below underline the inversion of the subject and the verb and circle the phrase which causes that inversion.

> Under no circumstances should you use that leg.

> At no time may dictionaries be used.

> Rarely have I come across such a terrible composition.

> Never have I seen anyone recover so quickly.

> Seldom have I seen anyone so ill.

> So bad was their work that they had to stay behind and do it again.

3 Now write a short and colourful paragraph about an imaginary and particularly unhealthy person. Use some of the phrases above.

Planning 2

Look at the exam question opposite. Use the table to help you organise your ideas. When you have finished compare your notes with a partner. Decide how you will organise your composition.

Exam question (Paper 2: discussion essay)

Why do you think people want to become doctors and nurses? (120–180 words)

Improving your work

Checking and polishing

Remember your time limit for checking in the exam. Check through your work within the time limit. Look particularly at the structure of your paragraphs and any inversions you have used.

Checking in the exam

In the exam, which mistakes are you particularly going to look out for? Look back over your last few compositions and note down what sort of mistakes you make most often.

In the exam you don't have very much time to check, so make sure you look especially at the areas where you are most likely to go wrong.

EXAM TIP 37

Check especially for the mistakes you know you make most often.

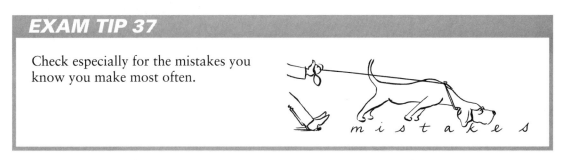

Unit 18　A birthday book

Planning technique:	review of planning techniques
Language skills:	making difficult choices; relative clauses
Exam question:	paper 3: directed writing
Improving:	the future

Preview

Discuss the following questions in pairs or small groups.

– When do you give presents in your family?
– When someone gives you a present do you open it in front of them or do you wait until later?
– When do you write to say 'thank you' for a present?
– Do you use a particular hand to give someone a present?
– When do you give someone flowers?
– What was the most disappointing present you ever had?
– What was the best present you ever had?
– Who do you find presents difficult to buy for?

Making difficult choices

Look at the information about these people. Choose one book for each of them.

1 Leo is 16. He is still at school.
2 Iain is 75. He is a retired policeman.
3 Jenny is 34. She owns a restaurant.

4 Kevin is 22. He is a gardener.
5 Isabelle is 53. She is President of an international travel company.
6 Harriet is 40. She is an art teacher.

a) *Grow Your Own Herbs*
b) *Gardens Throughout The World*
c) *Death Of An Artist* – an Inspector Lewis novel
d) *Your First Cookery Book*
e) *International Drug Smuggling – the true story!*
f) *A Concise History Of Art*

Compare your answers and your reasons. Were any of the decisions difficult to make? How did you decide?

EXAM TIP 38

In the directed writing question you may have to make decisions on the basis of a small amount of information. Choose a possibility you can justify.

CAN YOU JUSTIFY YOUR ANSWERS?

Relative clauses

1 Look at the sentences and underline the relative clauses.

a) The person who I have to buy a present for is called Leo.

b) Leo, who is still at school, would probably not like the spy thriller.

c) He would like the romance which I bought for my sister.

d) The book which would interest him the least is the one about gardening.

e) The travel book, which I have already read, is actually quite boring.

2 Answer the following questions.

a) In which sentences are there commas round the relative clause?
b) Which relative clauses contain **extra** information?
c) Which relative clauses contain **essential** information?

3 Now complete the top two lines of this table. Use your answers from question 2 to help you.

Type of relative clause (defining/non-defining) Sentence letters Extra information	.... **that** can be used instead of **who** or **which** relative pronoun can be omitted if it is the object of the relative clause no commas	.... **that** cannot be used relative pronoun cannot be omitted commas are used round the relative clause

4 Join each of the two sentences below into one sentence beginning with the words given and using a relative clause.

1 I would like to give Kevin the book about herbs. I saw it in the shop last week.

I would like ....

....

2 The gardening book is fascinating. I read it last month.

The gardening book ....

....

3 Iain is a retired policeman. He would love to read the book about drug smuggling.

Iain ....

....

➡

4 The woman would like a crime novel. She is President of her own company.

The woman ....

....

5 Leo would like one of the books. That's the one about cookery.

The book ....

....

Make sentences from the box below.

	love like 'm fond of 'm not very fond of don't like can't stand	people books films teachers drinks	which . . . that . . . who . . .
I			

Planning

Think back over the time you have been using this book and make a list of all the different techniques you have used to practise planning your compositions. Try and remember them all – but when you get stuck, have a look at the Contents page.

Is there any technique you use more than the others? If so, which? Are there any techniques you don't use? Compare and discuss your answers with a partner.

Read the exam question opposite and choose one or more of the techniques you have discussed to plan your answer.

EXAM TIP 39

Choose planning techniques which are appropriate to the exam question you choose to answer.

Exam question (Paper 3: directed writing)

Look at the information about the book below (or use your knowledge of the set book you have been studying) and answer the question in the space provided.

ELIZABETH JANE HOWARD

SOMETHING IN DISGUISE

A love story with a hint of the macabre–nor... stunning Tha... TV ser...

May's second marriage to Colonel Herbert Brown-Lacey is turning out to be a terrible mistake.

Her children find the colonel's presence oppressive and leave home; Oliver to drift from one affair to another, and Elizabeth to follow him to London in search of love and security. Even Herbert's own daughter, the shy and lonely Alice, is driven into marriage to escape from her father's sinister behaviour.

Elizabeth Jane Howard explores the personal and social interactions of this contemporary family with her customary candour and perception.

'Has all Elizabeth Jane Howard's particularly feminine perception... yet what lingers in the mind is its delicious funniness' William Trevor in the *Guardian*

The front cover illustration by Dave and Sue Holmes features (left to right) David Gwillim, Elizabeth Garvie and Anton Rodgers in the Thames Television serial *Something in Disguise*, produced and directed by Moira Armstrong from Elizabeth Jane Howard's dramatization of her own book. Executive Producer, John Frankau

United Kingdom £1.25
Australia $4.50 (recommended)
Canada $2.95

Fiction
ISBN 0 14
00,3288 6

What do you think the following people thought about either book?

Jack is 17. He is studying to get into university.

....

....

....

....

....

....

Kate is 42. She is a mother.

....

....

....

....

....

....

....

Lionel is 33. He is an estate agent.

....

....

....

....

....

....

You.

....

....

....

....

....

....

Improving your work

Checking and polishing

Remember your time limit for checking in the exam. Check through your work within that limit.

EXAM TIP 40

You should now feel confident about tackling the writing activities in the First Certificate. Remember what you have learnt and . . . Good luck!

The future

Where do you go from here? You probably won't stop learning English or learning to write English even if you have taken the First Certificate.

Work with a partner and discuss how you might continue learning English. Here are some suggestions:

- Enrol in another class.
- Think about taking a higher exam: Oxford Higher
                                                         Cambridge Advanced
                                                         Cambridge Proficiency
- Find a penfriend in an English-speaking country.
- Join a library which has English books and read one a month.
- Keep a diary in English.
- Study in an English-speaking country.
- Start an English newsletter with your friends.

Make two resolutions and write them below.

1 ....

2 ....

Review unit

How much do you know about the exam?

Are the following sentences *true* or *false*?

1 You have to write three compositions in Paper 2.
2 You are given 1½ hours to do Paper 2.
3 You can use English–English dictionaries.
4 One of the questions in Paper 2 could ask you to write a speech.
5 There might be a directed writing exercise in Paper 3.
6 You need to spend about 1½ hours on the directed writing exercise.
7 The examiners will count every mistake.
8 Each composition is marked out of 20.
9 8–11 marks is a 'pass'.
10 It's important to be aware of the number of words you write.

How much do you remember about planning?

In this book you have practised eleven different techniques for helping you to plan compositions. Some planning techniques will help you with particular types of composition. Match the technique on the left with the composition(s) on the right. The first one has been done for you.

flow diagram/order of events	discussion essays
order of priority	narratives
listing questions	discussion essays
'spidergraph'	directed writing / discussion essays
listing advantages and disadvantages	all types
questionnaires	descriptions / discussion essays
'brainstorming'	narratives
selecting points (and 'brainstorming')	directed writing / discussion essays
'headlights'	letters/speeches
opening sentences	all types
boxes	discussion essays

How much do you remember about the Exam Tips?

Work in pairs. Look at the key words and phrases opposite and together recall some of the advice given throughout the book. One has been done for you.

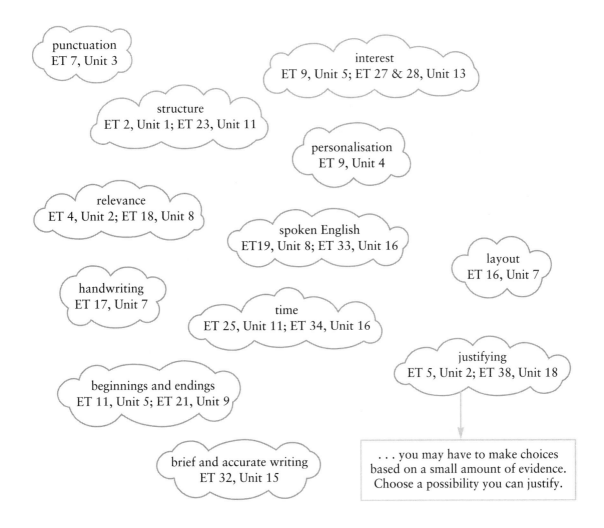

punctuation
ET 7, Unit 3

interest
ET 9, Unit 5; ET 27 & 28, Unit 13

structure
ET 2, Unit 1; ET 23, Unit 11

personalisation
ET 9, Unit 4

relevance
ET 4, Unit 2; ET 18, Unit 8

spoken English
ET19, Unit 8; ET 33, Unit 16

layout
ET 16, Unit 7

handwriting
ET 17, Unit 7

time
ET 25, Unit 11; ET 34, Unit 16

justifying
ET 5, Unit 2; ET 38, Unit 18

beginnings and endings
ET 11, Unit 5; ET 21, Unit 9

brief and accurate writing
ET 32, Unit 15

. . . you may have to make choices based on a small amount of evidence. Choose a possibility you can justify.

How prepared are you?

1 Look at the questions below. For each one:

a) identify the type of writing required
b) decide what planning technique(s) you would use

1 Write **two** paragraphs of about 75 words each outlining the advantages and disadvantages of having (i) a telephone and (ii) a credit card.
Having a telephone . . .
Possessing a credit card . . .

2 One of your classmates has won a scholarship to study at a university in the United States. You are asked to give a speech of congratulations. Write what you will say.

3 A parcel that was posted to you one month ago has not arrived. Write to the Post Office explaining the situation, describing the parcel and its contents, and saying where it was sent from.

4 Write a story beginning with the words: 'The moment we met I knew something extraordinary would happen.'

2 Now compare your answer with a partner. Then:

  a) note down any particular language you might need.
  b) plan the composition you would write.

How good are you at polishing your work?

The letter below was written in answer to the task in Unit 7. Look back at the question, read the letter and make whatever changes you think necessary to improve it.

Read through the letter again and note the good points about the letter.

19% Woodstock Road
Oxford OX2 7AB
England
12th February , 1992

University of Quebec
74 Queens Road
Quebec
3N4 5R6 CANADA

Dear Sir / Madam,

I am a Japanese student and have been studying English in England for four months. I would like to study computer and I heard that University of Quebec was very famous for its excellent curriculum and professors. Furthermore, my friend who has been in Canada recommends me your university.

I would really appreciate if you could send me more detail about computer course and other subjects. I had learned Turbo-Pascal at high school and I would like to learn programming.

I have never taken Cambridge examination and TOEFL. How much ability of English do I need at least if I go to your university? Do I need any certification such Cambridge Certificate or Proficiency? I would also like to know about that.

At last, I would also be grateful if you could tell me how much will it cost per year. I am going to apply for next year's course. I am sure that there are some student houses and I can live in one of them. I would like to know how much money I need totally. If it is possible, could you send me the detail as soon as possible.

I look forward to your reply.

Yours Faithfully,

(Miss) Sami Murata

FINAL TIP!

Don't panic in the exam!! You have practised all the language and writing skills you need. Stop and think! Use the skills you have learnt.